FORT WORTH

Energized for the Future

FORT WORTH

Energized for the Future

Broos Campbell, Vince Cummings, and Tina G. Rubin

Acknowledgements

Fort Worth: Energized for the Future was produced in cooperation with the Fort Worth Chamber of Commerce. Cherbo Publishing Group gratefully acknowledges its important contribution to this publication.

 cherbo publishing group, inc.

Cherbo Publishing Group, Inc.
Encino, California 91316
© 2012 by Cherbo Publishing Group, Inc.
All rights reserved. Published 2012.

Printed in Canada
By Friesens

ISBN: 978-1-882933-98-3

Library of Congress Cataloging-in-
Publication data
Campbell, B. D.
A pictorial guide highlighting
Fort Worth's economic sectors
and quality of life.
2012951206

Visit the CPG Web site at
www.cherbopub.com.

president	ELAINE HOFFMAN
editorial director	LINDA CHASE
creative director	PERI A. HOLGUIN
senior designer	THEODORE E. YEAGER
designer	NELSON CAMPOS
photo editors	KAREN MAZE, WALTER MLADINA
sales administrator	JOAN K. BAKER
senior project coordinator	PATRICIA DE LEONARD
client services coordinator	LESLIE E. SHAW
administrative assistant	BILL WAY
central regional manager	BOB FREEMAN

To purchase additional copies of this book, contact Joan Baker at Cherbo Publishing Group:
jbaker@cherbopub.com or phone 818.783.0040 ext. 27.

FORT WORTH

1867 CHISHOLM TRAIL 1875

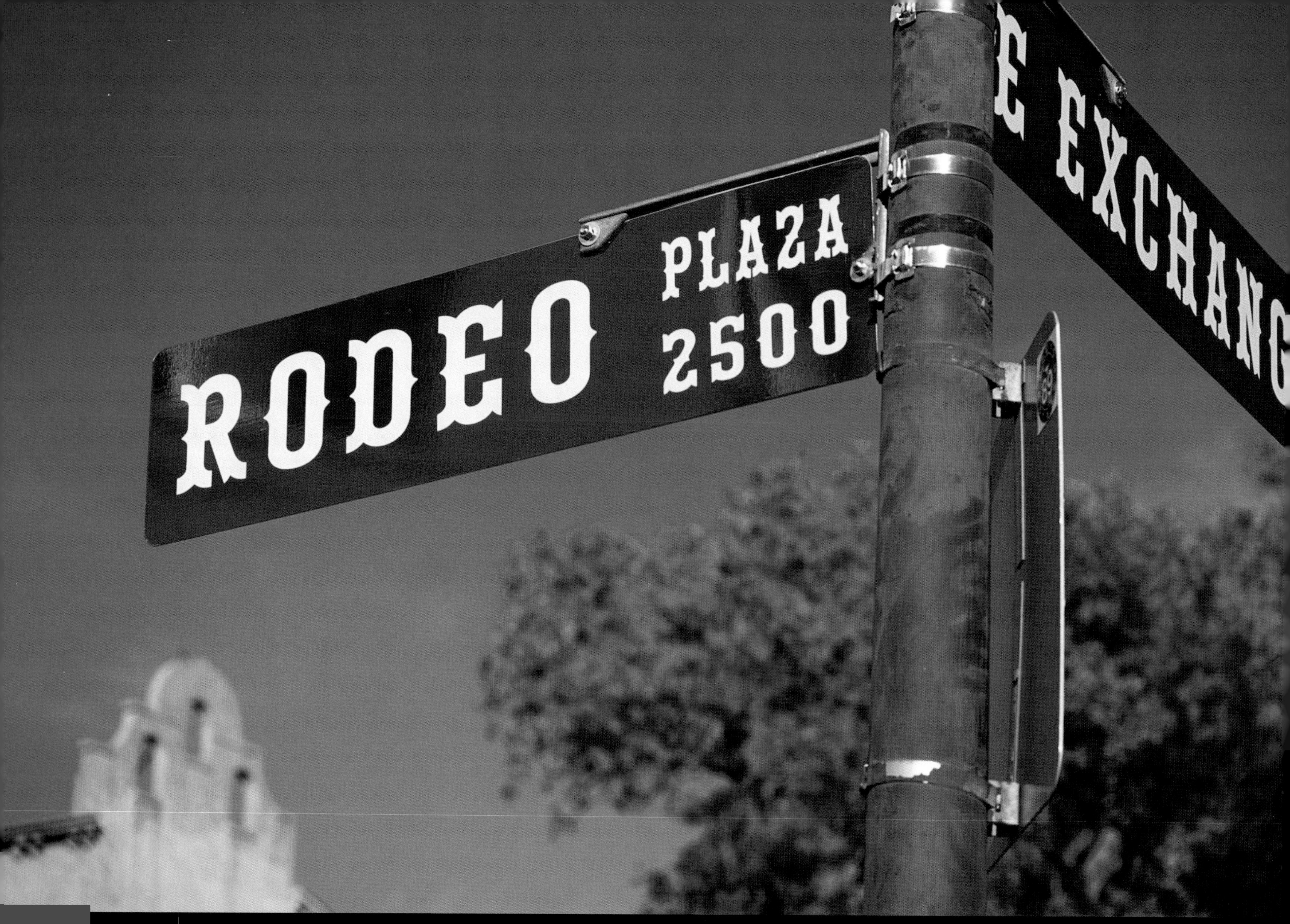
RODEO PLAZA
2500
E EXCHANG

CONTENTS

PROFILES IN EXCELLENCE

The following corporations and organizations, which are profiled in this publication, have displayed excellence in their fields and made a valuable contribution to the growth and success of the Fort Worth region.

BUSINESS VISIONARIES

The following companies and organizations are recognized as innovators in their fields and have played a prominent role in this publication, as they have in the Fort Worth region.

Bell Helicopter
P.O. Box 482
Fort Worth, TX 76101
Phone: 1.800.FLY.BELL
Fax: 1.817.280.2321
www.bellhelicopter.com
facebook.com/bellhelicopter
twitter.com/one_bell
On a Mission

BNSF Railway
2650 Lou Menk Drive
Fort Worth, TX 76131
Fax: 817.352.7925
www.bnsf.com
The Engine that Connects Us®

Cook Children's Health Care System
801 Seventh Avenue
Fort Worth, TX 76104
Phone: 682.885.4000
www.cookchildrens.org
facebook.com/cookchildrenshcs
twitter.com/cookchildrens

Dallas/Fort Worth International Airport
P.O. Box 619428
DFW Airport, TX 75261-9428
Phone: 972.973.5555
www.dfwairport.com
facebook.com/DFWAirport
twitter.com/dfwairport
The World Connected

Fort Worth Museum of Science and History
1600 Gendy Street
Fort Worth, TX 76107
Phone: 817.255.9300
Fax: 817.732.7635
www.fortworthmuseum.org
facebook.com/fwmsh
twitter.com/fwmsh
Dedicated to lifelong learning

Galderma Laboratories, L.P.
14501 North Freeway
Fort Worth, TX 76177
www.galdermausa.com
facebook.com/Cetaphil

National Farm Life Insurance
6001 Bridge Street
Fort Worth, TX 76112
Phone: 1.800.772.7557
Fax: 817.446.5181
www.nationalfarmlife.com

Pier 1 Imports
100 Pier 1 Place
Fort Worth, TX 76102
www.pier1.com
facebook.com/Pier1
twitter.com/Pier1

Tarrant County College
1500 Houston Street
Fort Worth, TX 76102
Phone: 817.515.TCCD (8223)
www.tccd.edu
Tomorrow Starts Here

UNT Health Science Center
3500 Camp Bowie Blvd.
Fort Worth, TX 76107
Phone: 817.735.2000
Fax: 817.735.0426
www.unthsc.edu
facebook.com/UNTHSC
twitter.com/unthsc
Where the best begins for health.

FOREWORD

Welcome to Fort Worth

As Mayor and a life-long resident of Cowtown, I'm proud to introduce *Fort Worth: Energized for the Future*. Our great city—"Where the West Begins"—celebrates both rugged independence and cultural refinement.

As a true Fort Worth cowgirl, I have ridden horses all my life and even barrel raced as a kid. But these days, a lot of us in Cowtown often trade our Western saddles for cycling saddles to enjoy Fort Worth's more than 60 miles of paved trails along the Trinity River. Fort Worth is truly authentic—we remain true to our Western heritage while pioneering progress and innovation.

The 16th-largest city in the nation, Fort Worth is endowed with a central location, diverse economy, and skilled workforce that make it a strong business magnet. We were once a modest oil and agriculture community at the gateway to the West. But today Fort Worth is the bustling home to industry leaders in aerospace, technology, life sciences, logistics, manufacturing, and energy. Our pro-business environment, safe neighborhoods, distinguished educational institutions (Go Frogs!), and low cost of living are among the many reasons why Fort Worth remains one of the fastest-growing large cities in the nation. People want to live here, and who can blame them? We really have it all here in Fort Worth!

In addition to being the perfect place to start or grow a career or business, Fort Worth is also an interesting and diverse entertainment destination. People flock to experience our rich mix of Western heritage, cultural gems, and progressive urban lifestyle. After all, where else can you see both a daily cattle drive and the only Michelangelo in the Western hemisphere? Or get fitted for a pair of custom cowboy boots before attending a performance by Yo-Yo Ma? While the range of experiences and entertainment Fort Worth offers is remarkable, it's our genuine Southern hospitality that you won't soon forget. As I said, we're authentic.

Fort Worth is a big Texas city with a small-town attitude, and all of us fortunate enough to call it home are truly energized for the future!

Betsy Price
Mayor, City of Fort Worth

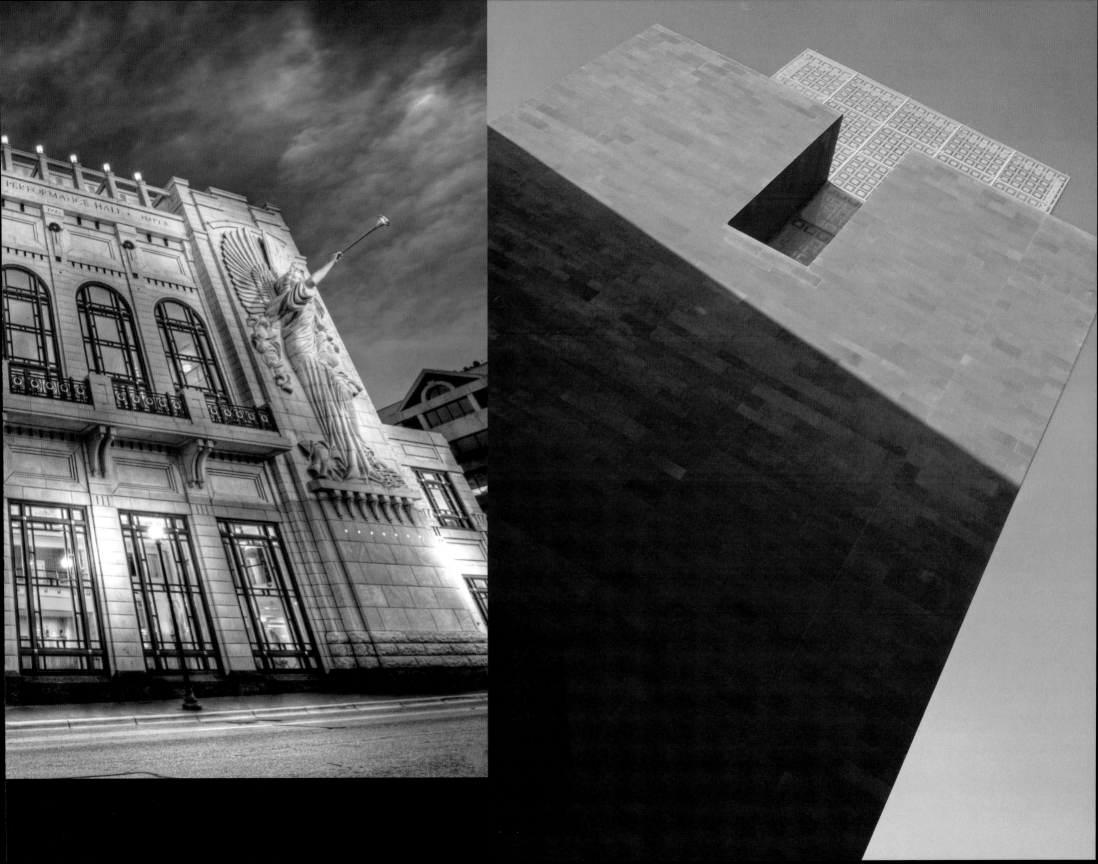

This spread: Cowboys and culture take center stage at Fort Worth museums. From left: A prop plane on exhibit at the American Airlines C.R. Smith Museum; Roxy Paine, *Conjoined*, 2007, a stainless-steel sculpture outside the Modern Art Museum of Fort Worth; the Texas Cowboy Hall of Fame in the Stockyards.

This spread: Spectator sports enjoy a huge fan base in Fort Worth. Left to right: The NASCAR Sprint Cup Samsung Mobile 500 trophy at Texas Motor Speedway; the Dallas Cowboys battle the Chicago Bears at Cowboys Stadium in Arlington; Yu Darvish (11) takes the field for the Texas Rangers at Rangers Ballpark in Arlington.

This spread: Fort Worth is a year-round outdoor paradise. From left: Enjoying the zen-like tranquility of the Japanese Garden at the Fort Worth Botanic Garden; exploring the lush vegetation at the Fort Worth Nature Center; biking the Trinity River Trail.

FORT WORTH TIMELINE

1849　　1873　　1884　　1896

The Tarantula Train, a late-19th-century locomotive out of Fort Worth

1849 Major Ripley A. Arnold and a troop of soldiers set up a fort on the Trinity River to protect early settlers from Native American attacks. The fort is named for Major General William J. Worth, a hero of the Mexican War.

1853 The U.S. Army abandons Fort Worth for new posts further west, and pioneer settlers already in the area claim it as their permanent home.

1854 The first public school in town is established by John Peter Smith in an abandoned army hospital. Smith's importance in the community earns him the nickname the "Father of Fort Worth."

1860 After a long and bitter fight known as the County Seat War, Fort Worth becomes the home of government for Tarrant County.

1866 Fort Worth, a stopping point for cowboys herding cattle along the Chisholm Trail, earns the nickname "Cowtown." Growth and prosperity as a cattle trading center help the town recover from post–Civil War shortages.

1873 The Texas and Pacific Railroad agrees to a charter that will bring a railroad through town.

1873 W. P. Burts is elected Fort Worth's first mayor.

1876 The tracks in Fort Worth are completed and the Texas and Pacific Railway arrives, turning the city into a transit point for cattle shipments and wholesale trade.

1878 The Yuma Stage Line makes regular stops in Fort Worth, which will become the eastern terminus for the route to Yuma, Arizona.

Stagecoach departs Fort Worth, ca. 1870s

1883 Fort Worth's first hospital, the Missouri Pacific Hospital, is built to serve the health care needs of railroad workers. In 1930 its name is changed to St. Joseph Hospital.

1884 Local businessmen establish Fort Worth National Bank, originally named Tidball, Van Zandt, and Company.

1889 As part of the town's strategy for continued growth and commercial expansion, the Texas Spring Palace opens as an educational, cultural, and entertainment center designed to attract both settlers and investors.

1892 The State of Texas grants a charter to establish the Fort Worth Public Library Association, which is devoted to the "accumulation of paintings and artistic work." Many years later the Modern Art Museum of Fort Worth (the Modern) is a thriving cultural landmark.

1896 The first livestock show in Fort Worth is held near Marine Creek. The event later becomes known as the Fat Stock Show, a world-famous livestock exhibition and rodeo.

1903 Attracted by financial incentives, railroads, and abundant cattle, the Armour and Swift meat packing companies decide to open plants in Fort Worth.

1908 The Cowtown Coliseum, completed at a cost of $250,000, holds the country's first exhibition cattle roundup conducted under a roof.

1908 1917 1920 1925

Student pilot with instructor at Meacham Field, 1942

1917 Construction of Camp Bowie, named after the Alamo hero James Bowie, begins three miles west of downtown. The camp trains the 36th Infantry Division for 10 months before the soldiers are shipped to France.

1917 Oil gushes from a well on the McCleskey Farm west of Fort Worth, bringing economic prosperity and helping to meet the fuel demands of World War I.

1920 Five working refineries tap Fort Worth's underground oil reserves, making the city a center for oil activity and turning many ranchers and farmers into millionaires. Luxury homes and office buildings follow the newly found wealth.

1925 The Fort Worth Municipal Airport is established, and two years later is named Meacham Field after the town's former mayor.

1930 The Fort Worth Panthers (precursor of the Cats) baseball team wins the Texas League Crown.

1908 The Southwestern Baptist Theological Seminary is established. It will become one of the largest seminaries in the world.

1909 The Fort Worth Zoo opens.

1911 A dam constructed on the West Fork River creates Lake Worth, a reliable water supply and at the time the largest municipal water-supply reservoir in Texas.

1918 The Southwestern Exposition and Fat Stock Show holds the world's first indoor rodeo—increasing the event's attendance considerably and becoming the high point of the year for thousands of people.

1922 Fort Worth resident and newspaper owner Amon G. Carter Sr. establishes WBAP, Fort Worth's first radio station, which will become one of the few 50,000-watt clear-channel stations in the country. It is also the first radio station to broadcast livestock market reports and weekly church services.

1936 The Texas Centennial Frontier—celebrating the 100-year anniversary of the Republic of Texas—is held in Fort Worth. Sponsored by Amon G. Carter, Sr., at a cost of $5 million, it depicts life on the frontier.

1941 Fort Worth Museum of Science and History opens; it is the first children's museum in Texas and one of the first such museums in the country.

FORT WORTH TIMELINE

1941   1959   1991   2001

1941 The Consolidated Aircraft Company announces the construction of a $10 million plant near Fort Worth to build four-motor bombers. The main building of the factory covers 30 acres.

1942 After the attack on Pearl Harbor in December 1941, Tarrant Field is assigned to the Army Air Forces Flying Training Command. The base serves as a pilot transition school and aircraft factory throughout World War II and is named Carswell Air Force Base in 1948.

1948 The first commercial television station in Texas—WBAP-TV—begins in Fort Worth. The station's first broadcast is of a speech given by President Harry Truman.

1959 The Fort Worth Independent School District is chosen as the home of a special laboratory for superior science students that will be funded by grants from the National Institutes of Health.

1962 The first Van Cliburn International Piano Competition is held in Fort Worth, with $10,000 going to the first-place winner.

1973 The Dallas/Fort Worth International Airport opens. It is the largest airport in the United States at the time.

1991 The United States Bureau of Engraving and Printing holds the official opening of its Western Currency Facility in Fort Worth, chosen from 80 cities as the site for printing U.S. currency.

1992 The Fort Worth Zoo reopens after numerous improvements throughout. Attendance reaches one million visitors that year.

The Smoking Signal, Frederick Remington, 1905

A riveter at Consolidated Aircraft

1956 Elvis Presley entertains 7,000 fans at the Cowtown Coliseum.

1958 Van Cliburn, a Fort Worth native, wins the first annual Tchaikovsky International Competition in Moscow; Premier Khrushchev gives the judges his personal permission to award the prize to an American.

The Fort Worth Rodeo becomes the first rodeo to receive live national television coverage, on NBC-TV. Roy Rogers and Dale Evans host the show.

1984 Texas-born George Strait's country-western song "Does Fort Worth Ever Cross Your Mind?" strikes a chord with millions of listeners, topping the Billboard chart; the recording wins the Country Music Association's Album of the Year award in 1985.

1986 Sundance Square, the centerpiece of a downtown improvement project, will develop into a vibrant 20-block entertainment and commercial area featuring shops, restaurants, nightclubs, and high-rise living.

1998 Bass Performance Hall opens. The crown jewel of the downtown revitalization project, it is the permanent home of the Fort Worth Symphony Orchestra, Texas Ballet Theater, Fort Worth Opera, and Van Cliburn International Piano Competition.

1998 Fort Worth is ranked number one on *Money* magazine's list of the South's Most Livable Places.

2001 The Amon Carter Museum opens after a $39 million expansion that triples its exhibit space. The new museum houses Carter's large collection of sculptures by Frederic Remington and Charles M. Russell, as well as 19th- and 20th-century paintings, photographs, and graphic arts.

2002 A record 951,000 people attend the Fort Worth Stock Show.

2002   2004   2011   2012

2002 The National Cowgirl Museum and Hall of Fame relocates to a new facility in Fort Worth's Cultural District. The museum is the only one in the world that honors the pioneer women of the American West.

2003 The Fort Worth Convention Center gets a $75 million renovation, making the facility a premier 21st-century venue for shows and exhibits.

2004 By sustaining a high-quality of life for its citizens and maximizing the value of the community's assets, Fort Worth earns recognition as one of America's Most Livable Communities by Partners for Livable Communities.

2005 Nearly six million passengers travel through Dallas/Fort Worth International Airport, making it the sixth-busiest airport in the world by number of passengers.

2006 Dallas/Fort Worth International Airport is named "The Best Cargo Airport in the World" by *Air Cargo World* magazine in its Air Cargo Excellence Survey.

Dallas/Fort Worth International Airport

2003 The Fort Worth City Council adopts a Master Plan for an 88-mile stretch of the Trinity River. The plan calls for expanded parks, trails, water recreation, environmental preservation, and commercial and residential development in the heart of the city.

2008 The classical music world commemorates the 50th anniversary of Van Cliburn's win at the Tchaikovsky International Piano Competition in 1958.

2009 New Cowboys Stadium opens. Soaring 292 feet above the playing field, two monumental arches support a retractable roof—the world's longest single-span roof structure.

2011 Fort Worth is named an All-American City by the National Civic League.

Fort Worth is the fastest-growing major metropolitan area in U.S., according to U.S. Census Bureau.

2012 USS *Fort Worth* becomes first U.S. naval vessel to bear the name of a city.

New Sundance Square Plaza opens in downtown Fort Worth.

A new JFK Tribute is unveiled on the site of the president's last public speech on Nov. 23, 1963.

Chisholm Trail Parkway opens. More than 40 years in the making, the 27.6-mile toll road extends from downtown Fort Worth south to Cleburne.

Above: These handmade Leddys cowboy boots are on display at the Historic Stockyards in Fort Worth.

COWBOYS AND CULTURE

PART ONE

Above, from left: Designed by Philip Johnson, the Fort Worth Water Gardens is a refreshing oasis adjacent to the Fort Worth Convention Center; Maverick Fine Western Wear is located in a 1905 building in the Stockyards District.

Western Style

BOOTS

MAVERICK
Fine Western Wear

MAVERICK
BUILDING
ERECTED
1905

CHAPTERONE

Fort Worth

FROM FRONTIER OUTPOST TO MODERN METROPOLIS

On June 6, 1849, Major Ripley Arnold established an outpost on the banks of the Trinity River and called it Camp Worth. A treaty with the Native Americans drew a line signifying "Where the West Begins." This now-famous slogan was to prove an apt description for Fort Worth, which became a stop along the Chisholm Trail for the cattle drives and later became a rail shipping point for stock.

More than a century later, Fort Worth was honored for its Western roots and uniquely American character when the USS *Fort Worth* became the first combatant vessel in U.S. naval history to bear the name of a city. Commissioned in Galveston in the fall of 2012, the ship bears a laurel wreath crest emblazoned with the Texas longhorn symbolizing the city and its nickname "Cowtown." Placed on the mast is a button from a cavalry dragoon's uniform found near the site of the original fort in the late 1840s.

While the USS *Fort Worth* embarks on its first mission, the City of Fort Worth continues on its mission of creating a vibrant, sustainable urban environment that is the envy of the world. Steeped in Western heritage, the city has emerged in the 21st century as a thriving metropolitan hub of business and culture. Currently the 16th-most-populous American city, Fort Worth is home to 740,000 people, with census data projecting approximately a 60 percent growth by 2030. Residents enjoy a vibrant quality of life that features world-class museums, upscale shops and restaurants, and year-round sports and recreation.

Once overshadowed by its larger neighbor to the east, Fort Worth has achieved a stature that complements Dallas and the region, economically and culturally. Linked by the Trinity River Express Rail and sharing DFW International Airport, the two cities are good-natured rivals that come together to cheer for their sports teams. In 2011 football fans flocked to the newly opened Cowboys Stadium for Super Bowl XLV. Rangers Ballpark in Arlington is home to the AL West powerhouse that played in back-to-back World Series in 2010 and 2011.

A Diverse Economy

Economic diversity has fueled the region's remarkable growth over the past 20 years. Several Fortune 500 companies are headquartered here, among them such notable names such as RadioShack and Pier 1 Imports. Leading industry sectors in the region include aerospace, health care, transportation, communications, manufacturing, construction, and gas and petroleum products. Leading

employers in the region include American Airlines/AMR, with more than 22,000 employees; Texas Health Resources, with more than 18,800; and Lockheed Martin, with nearly 15,000.

The economic engine of the city, the Downtown Central Business District (CBD) had an employment base of more than 52,000 persons in 2011 according to the U.S. Census Bureau. This urban center offers 11 million square feet of office space, along with first-class hotels, restaurants, shops, arts and entertainment venues, and historic structures. Spanning a 14-block area in the heart of downtown, the recently renovated Fort Worth Convention Center is a state-of-the-art facility featuring a total of 253,226 square feet of exhibit space and business services, including free WiFi in all public areas. The center is within easy walking distance of downtown attractions. Nearby accommodations range from historic hotels such as the prestigious Fort Worth Club, founded in 1885, to the opulent

Worthington Renaissance Fort Worth Hotel, which was renovated in 2007, and the striking new Omni Fort Worth Hotel, which is adjacent to the center.

To preserve the charm of downtown, the city established the Downtown Design Review Board (DDRB) to review projects and ensure adherence to the Downtown Urban Design Standards. The Fort Worth Improvement District #1 (PID), which was renewed for 20 years, provides a wide range of vital services, including daily sidewalk cleaning, trash removal, and weekly street-sweeping service. The Downtown PID provides funding for year-round blooms in the 17,000 square feet of planters. Working directly with the City of Fort Worth and other local agencies, the PID also funds transportation and planning efforts; it even furnishes supplies for the mounted patrol.

North of downtown, combined public and private investment has spurred development of key infrastructure at the 17,000-acre AllianceTexas development, including a large general-aviation airport, water and wastewater facilities, and highway improvements. Augmenting the nearly $6.8 billion in private investment were $388 million in local, state, and federal funds. AllianceTexas has generated a $38.5 billion economic impact for the North Texas region since 1990, and is home to more than 300 companies and nearly 31,000 employees.

Foreign-Trade Zone No. 196 at Alliance is ranked No. 1 among U.S. general-purpose FTZs for value of foreign merchandise admitted to the zone. Major users of Foreign-Trade Zone No. 196 include Hyundai, Trans-Trade, LEGO, GENCO ATCLE, Callaway, and Motorola.

This page: The Fort Worth Convention Center fronts Houston Street. Opposite page: These famous logos sit outside the Fort Worth headquarters of RadioShack (left) and American Airlines.

21

The Mercantile Center, a 1,500-acre master-planned business park in north Fort Worth, is home to Tech Center VII, with 80,000 square feet of flex/tech space. Mercantile Partners, the developer for Mercantile Center, has launched an expansion to add state-of-the-art office/warehouse buildings called Mercantile Distribution Center 5 and 6 that will further enhance the region's robust distribution sector.

Entrepreneurs and business owners can turn to financial incentive programs that include everything from economic program development grants for developers to the Fort Worth Business Assistance Center's aid for start-ups and small business owners. TECH Fort Worth, a nonprofit business incubator, helps entrepreneurs develop and market innovative technologies that will help improve the environment, empower the community, and enhance the quality of health care. A public-private partnership of the UNT Health Science Center at Fort Worth, the City of Fort Worth, and the North Texas business community, TECH launched Fort Worth Cowtown Angels, a program to connect high-performance, technology-based start-ups with investors in North Texas. The program will serve as a springboard for new ventures in such vital high-tech sectors as software development, health care, and energy.

To provide capital for small businesses in the Fort Worth area, Southwest Bank, the largest locally owned independent commercial bank in Tarrant County, received an investment loan of $29.8 million under the U.S. Treasury Small Business Lending Fund. The Bank of Texas provides intermediary financing to small businesses that have historically not had ready access to capital markets, enabling them to grow and succeed. Cash America offers a variety of financial services, from loans to insurance and tax filing.

Professional services from insurance to legal counsel are provided by leading Fort Worth firms. Founded in Fort Worth in 1946 to provide life insurance for professional agriculture workers, National Farm Life Insurance today has almost $2.3 billion of life insurance in force throughout Texas. Jackson Walker, a Texas-based law firm with a Fort Worth office, provides legal services for 76 of the Fortune 500 companies and six of the Fortune 10.

Fort Worth can be justly proud of its diversity in the business community. One example is Open Channels Group, a woman- and minority-owned public relations agency based in downtown Fort Worth. OCG serves a growing list of clients representing a range of industries, from energy and health care to sports and family entertainment.

Education and Urban Living

Education in the Fort Worth area includes outstanding public and private schools from preschool through grade 12. The city's public school systems are lauded in Sperling's Best Places for their excellent library and counseling services, boasting more of these resources per student than the national average. Among Fort Worth's many excellent private schools is the Fort Worth Academy of Fine Arts, which enjoys a Gold national ranking on *U.S. News & World Report*'s Best High Schools survey.

Beyond senior year, colleges and universities in Fort Worth and the Metroplex offer a wide variety of superb programs. Texas Christian University (TCU) has been touted by *U.S. News & World Report*, *Forbes*, and the Carnegie Commission, among others, as a top-tier university, with outstanding business and journalism schools.

The Central Business District is home to several campuses. Tarrant County College's Trinity River East Campus, which opened in 2011, is built into the bluff overlooking the river. The new University of Texas at Arlington Fort Worth Center and Texas Wesleyan Law School, which will become the Texas A&M School of Law at Texas Wesleyan University in 2013, are also located here.

A strong education system is only part of the appeal of Fort Worth, which is undergoing a renaissance in urban living through its revitalized urban villages.

Sperling's Best Places lauded Fort Worth for its lower cost of living, less expensive housing, and property taxes that are lower than the national average. The median home price in Fort Worth in 2012 was around $115,000, most affordable in comparison to many U.S. metropolitan areas. Residents can choose from a wide range of housing options, from apartments and condos in renovated urban villages to riverfront townhomes with scenic views to master-planned communities with room for growing families. Williams Trew Sotheby's International Realty, based in Fort Worth, provides access to luxury listings in north-central Texas and throughout the Southeast.

Whether you are a newcomer or longtime resident, business owner or arts aficionado, you will find Fort Worth to be a diverse, dynamic city, one that is mindful of its rich heritage, yet, like its naval namesake, is charting a bold course to the future.

Above, from left: Downtown Fort Worth dazzles at twilight; *Man With Briefcase*, a sculpture by Jonathan Borofsky, soars over Burnett Plaza in downtown Fort Worth.

Cityscape

TEXAS ROOTS MEET URBAN INNOVATION

From a series of bluffs overlooking the scenic Trinity River, a low-slung skyline to the south is marked by grand historic structures and the glimmer and sheen of postmodern facades.

This is Fort Worth, a city that is continually improving while staying true to its deep Texas roots. From the 570-foot Burnett Plaza to the 1885 Fort Worth Club and 1907 Flatiron Building, the city center is a quick survey course in the history of Fort Worth and North Texas. From here, throughout the many neighborhoods of the city and to the outlying landscape that is characterized by majestic, sprawling lands, the Fort Worth metro area is a vibrant and welcoming environment for residents and visitors alike.

Enjoying pride of place in the heart of downtown Fort Worth, Sundance Square features the Burk Burnett Building and the former Woolworth's Building, both on the National Register of Historic Buildings. Crowning Sundance Square is the long-awaited new plaza, whose performance pavilion and interactive fountain will create a focal point for this beautiful area. Umbrellas on the east side of the plaza create an inviting setting during the day, and at night LED lighting bathes the entire scene in an inviting glow. Several new retail buildings surround the plaza, and the Worthington Renaissance Fort Worth Hotel affords a view of the square, making this a true downtown hot spot.

CHAPTER**TWO**

General Worth Square, a 1.5-acre park north of the convention center, is the site where President Kennedy delivered a breakfast address prior to his departure to Dallas on November 22, 1963. Marking this overlooked moment in U.S. history is the JFK Tribute, which opened in the square in 2012. This moving homage, which was funded by $2 million in corporate and private donations, features an eight-foot bronze sculpture of JFK created by Texas sculptor Lawrence Ludtke. Larger-than-life photos depict the president's visit to Fort Worth, and an exhibit recounts the events of that fateful morning.

Perhaps the city's best-known landmark is the Fort Worth Stockyards. Beginning in 1876, this area served as a livestock center for the new railroad. Today this historic district is listed on the National Register. Entertainment and retail mix with dozens of historic buildings to create a true Fort Worth experience. The Fort Worth Stockyards Stables, located in a 1912 structure, offer the opportunity to board or even rent horses to ride through the Stockyards area and along the Trinity.

The stellar museums located in the Cultural District have put Fort Worth on the national arts and culture map. The Amon Carter Museum of American Art, the

Kimbell Art Museum, the Modern Art Museum of Fort Worth, the Fort Worth Museum of Science and History, and the National Cowgirl Museum and Hall of Fame form the nucleus of art and science venues in the area. The Will Rogers Memorial Center, located in the heart of the Cultural District, hosts numerous equestrian, cultural, and recreational events, including the Fort Worth Stock Show and Rodeo. A newcomer to the district is the Botanical Research Institute of Texas.

Urban Villages

In 2002 Fort Worth launched its pioneering Urban Village Development Program. A collaboration of developers, business groups, and neighborhood associations, this innovative approach to urban living uses a combination of capital improvements, mixed-use zoning, and economic incentives to transform vital pockets of the city into dynamic micro-communities that emphasize local culture and heritage. Usually no more than a square mile, these "cities within a city" are mass-transit and pedestrian friendly, featuring parks, businesses, retail, entertainment, and residences—all within easy walking distance of each other.

This page: World-renowned architect Tadao Ando designed the Modern Art Museum of Fort Worth. Opposite page, from left: A patron views a painting at the Kimbell Art Museum; a cowboy and longhorn pose for a photo at the Fort Worth Stockyards.

Above, from left: This Fort Worth food truck park is a foodies' paradise; Fort Worth has its own Flatiron Building, a steel-frame structure completed in 1907 at the corner of Houston and West 9th.

A total of 16 urban villages have emerged from this urban rebirth. The Near Southside, directly south of downtown, encompasses the Hospital District, with more than 30,000 residents working in medical institutions here. This walkable district is about more than merely health care, however, with historic architecture throughout, including the 1920s ABC Flag Co. and the Iron House, dating back to 1910.

Magnolia Village, located within the district, is part of the urban village program. Streetscaping and other improvements create a Main Street feel here, with ample office space, retail, and housing. Freese and Nichols, an engineering and architectural consulting firm, provided planning and design for Hemphill Street to create a pedestrian-friendly streetscape with landscape features, sidewalk enhancements, roadway, and intersection improvements, with crosswalks, street lighting, and parallel parking.

Six Points, just southeast of downtown, centers around the restaurants and nightlife on Race Street. The historic McAdams building serves as a focal point for this lively area. The Near East Side also attracts visitors with its combination of offices, housing, and retail, in addition to its proximity to downtown.

The Upper West Side, at the edge of the CBD, combines chic, upscale urban residences with tony professional buildings and is a stone's throw away from West 7th Street.

Westover Hills is Fort Worth's premier neighborhood, with the highest per-capita income in Texas. Located north of Camp Bowie Boulevard and next to the Shady Oaks Country Club several miles west of downtown, Westover Hills features sumptuous mansions, some of which date back to the early 20th century, and architect-designed, custom-built residences on tree-lined streets.

Arlington Heights, adjacent to the Cultural District, also offers many historic homes, dating back to the 1920s. Bungalows and Tudor-style houses are prevalent here. Arlington Heights' residents include families, young professionals, and retirees, who love the area for its character as well as its central location.

Residential Rivercrest, west of downtown and north of Camp Bowie Boulevard, has everything from old mansions to stylish apartments, with bungalows and Tudors as well. Newer mansions also attract residents to the neighborhood, which surrounds the exclusive Rivercrest Country Club.

Fairmount, just southwest of downtown, is a residential neighborhood with a wealth of historic homes dating from the 1880s to about 1910. There is even a community garden here where anyone with a green thumb can work in the dirt. The Historic Southside also includes Mistletoe, Berkeley, and Ryan Place.

Throughout the city's many neighborhoods and urban villages, storied structures and classic facades comprise a rich saga. Historic Fort Worth is a nonprofit organization that helps to interpret this tale through education and ensure its retelling through preservation of the city's beloved architecture. Since 1969, Historic Fort Worth has been leading the way with programs that include the Economic Incentives Training for Developers of Historic Properties, Facade Easement Program, and many more. In addition, the groundbreaking organization conducts citywide tours that are inspiring and fun, including a Hidden Gardens Tour of Fort Worth, Designer Showhouses, and many others.

Historic Fort Worth owns several properties, which it operates and restores and even makes available to the public for private events. One such property, the 1899 Ball-Eddleman-McFarland House, also houses the Preservation Resource Center, where architecture buffs and the preservation-minded can research topics that are vital in bringing the past into the future.

One of the city's most intriguing attractions is Fort Worth Heritage Trails. This self-guided walking tour gives visitors details of fascinating historic events

that occurred right here, from "Longhair Jim" Courtright's fated gunfight with casino owner Luke Short in 1887 to JFK's final public appearance. The Heritage Trail Walking Map, available at the Fort Worth Convention & Visitors Bureau and several other places throughout the district, indicates sites throughout the neighborhood where bronze plaques mark each historic site.

From historic sites to modern urban villages, downtown skyscrapers and lofts to attractive suburbs, the Fort Worth area combines the intimacy and scalability of a small-town environment with the cultural assets and other amenities of a thriving metropolis.

This page, from left: Visitors pause before a Heritage Trail map; the historic Ball-Eddleman-McFarland House, a cattle baron's mansion, completed in 1904, features hand-carved sandstone and a wrap-around porch. Opposite page: River Crest Country Club, Fort Worth's oldest country club, opened in 1911.

31

Above, from left: Raymond Nasher, founder of the Nasher Sculpture Center, studies a work from the "Anselm Kiefer: Heaven and Earth" exhibit at the Modern Art Museum of Fort Worth; the cuisine at Bonnell's of Fort Worth is both down-home and upscale.

FROM HIGH ART TO COOL CUISINE

Ever since a tall young Texan named Van Cliburn went to Moscow and brought home first prize in the Tchaikovsky Competition, Fort Worth culture lovers have had ample reason to be proud of their hometown. From the annual Van Cliburn International Piano Competition held at Bass Performance Hall to the world-renowned museums found in the Cultural District, Fort Worth has earned a place among the great cultural capitals of the world.

Anchoring the Cultural District is the Kimbell Art Museum, a Louis Kahn–designed structure that itself is a work of art. The highly regarded collection includes works by Michelangelo, Caravaggio, El Greco, Gauguin, and other landmark European artists, along with many outstanding Asian artworks, adding up to a collection that is one of the finest in the nation.

An expansion of the museum includes a separate structure designed by noted architect Renzo Piano, scheduled for completion by 2013. Lectures and public programs, plus school and teacher programs and family activities, enhance the Kimbell Art Museum's value to the city.

CHAPTER**THREE**

The adjacent Amon Carter Museum of American Art is a veritable history lesson in American art, with artworks by Thomas Cole, Stuart Davis, Winslow Homer, Georgia O'Keeffe, John Singer Sargent, and others. In addition, a dedicated education department reaches out to individuals and local educators alike to enrich the entire community.

A significant collection that boasts the names of such modern and postmodern giants as Picasso, Pollock, and Warhol is on display at the Modern Art Museum of Fort Worth, which has the second-largest modern-art gallery space after MoMA in New York. Musical performances, film series, lectures, and more make this a one-stop art destination.

Located in Sundance Square, the Sid Richardson Museum comprises an outstanding collection of paintings by Frederic Remington, Charles M. Russell, and other artists. Set in a replica of an 1895 building, the museum offers inspiring Western art in perfect surroundings. After a tour of the museum, patrons can stroll among Sundance Square's restored turn-of-the-century buildings and enjoy a glimpse of the splashy new plaza.

The 1902 Livestock Exchange Building, one of Fort Worth's oldest commercial buildings, is home to the popular Stockyards Museum. Inside is a wealth of informational exhibits about the region's cattle-ranching culture, including background on African American and Hispanic cowboys. Visitors love the museum's 1908 Palace Theater Light Bulb, which has burned for more than a century.

Fort Worth just may be the perfect city for the National Cowgirl Museum and Hall of Fame. Located in the Cultural District, this shrine to the likes of Patsy Cline, Annie Oakley, Dale Evans Rogers, and even Sandra Day O'Connor features multimedia displays about rodeo heroines and pop-culture icons. There's also a hands-on play area for kids.

Cowboys get equal time at the Texas Cowboy Hall of Fame in the Fort Worth Stockyards National Historic District. Bull riders, leading men, musicians, and major league pitchers are among the honorees—Tommy Lee Jones, George Strait, and Nolan Ryan are just a few of the figures in the Hall. A kids' exploratorium instructs aspiring cowboys with tutorials on the importance of branded cattle and how to stock a chuckwagon.

This page: The National Cowgirl Museum and Hall of Fame. Opposite page, from left: The Livestock Exchange Building in the Historic Fort Worth Stockyards; the Sid Richardson Museum in Sundance Square.

This page: A dinosaur skeleton at the Fort Worth Museum of Science and History. Opposite page: An architectural detail of an angel on the facade of the Bass Performance Hall.

The American Airlines C.R. Smith Museum, located at the American Airlines Flight Academy on the edge of DFW International Airport, is a fascinating tribute to the air-travel industry. Full-scale aircraft engines, photo exhibits, and historical artifacts engage visitors of all ages. In the museum's digital theater, visitors get a close look at aviation history with *The Spirit of America*, a film that boasts incredible aerial photography.

For anyone fascinated with science, the Fort Worth Museum of Science and History offers the Omni IMAX theater and Noble Planetarium, plus changing exhibits that provide a close look at everything from the Mesozoic Age to the universe beyond. Learning opportunities include programs for educators and adults, as well as such outreach programs as Astronomy on Wheels.

Sounds of the City

Beautiful Bass Hall, located downtown, is home to the Fort Worth Symphony Orchestra, which celebrated its centennial season in 2012 and performs symphonic and pops concerts. Bass Hall is also the local performance venue for the Texas Ballet Theater, a resident company of Fort Worth and Dallas.

The esteemed Fort Worth Opera, also headquartered in Bass Hall, performs three to four operas per year in a popular festival format. It is the oldest continually performing opera company in Texas, and among the oldest in the nation. The organization's dedication to the community is evident in the Children's Opera Tour, which brings opera to some 100,000 children per year throughout the Lone Star State.

Fewer places are more fun for kicking up your heels than Fort Worth. There's twangy country music, rock, jazz, and comedy among the city's generous sampling of entertainment. A popular Stockyards performance venue, Billy Bob's is a famous Texas landmark that has been the setting for numerous movies and TV shows over the years, from the original *Dallas* series and *Walker, Texas Ranger* with Chuck Norris to *Rhinestone* with Dolly Parton and Sylvester Stallone.

Lone Star in Sundance Square is a great place to enjoy entertainment of all description. There's a comedy stage, dueling pianos, karaoke, a dance club with a DJ and live bands most nights, which makes this 22,000-square-foot venue an all-in-one Fort Worth nightlife emporium.

Flavors of Fort Worth

Fort Worth figured prominently at Lyndon Johnson's first state dinner as president. Held barely a month after the assassination of JFK, the dinner was not the usual formal White House affair; instead, it was a chuck-wagon-style barbecue held at the LBJ Ranch. Leaving nothing to chance, LBJ flew in Walter Jetton, a caterer from Fort Worth, to supervise the food preparation. According to Lady Bird's diary, the menu featured "beans (pinto beans, always), delicious barbecued spareribs, cole slaw, followed by fried apricot pies with lots of hot coffee. And plenty of beer." The coffee was Jetton's famous six-shooter brew, which one Texan said was "so strong it will float a .44." The guest of honor, West German Chancellor Ludwig Erhard, was charmed by the down-home flavor of the food and the entertainment. The latter was supplied by another Fort Worth native, Van Cliburn, who had won world renown with his triumphant victory at the Tchaikovsky Competition.

In North Texas, barbecue is king. Off-the-Bone in Forest Hill and Angelo's, Riscky's, and Smokey's in Fort Worth are among the highly regarded "hot" spots for 'cue. Chef Tim Love applies his love of all things smoked at The Woodshed Smokehouse.

Mexican cuisine is also found in plentiful supply in Fort Worth. Salsa Fuego was named among the top five Mexican restaurants in the state by *Texas Monthly*. A Northside institution, Joe T. Garcia's serves up old-school combination plates and margaritas in a courtyard setting. Garcia's great-grandson Lanny has put his own stamp on authentic Mexican cuisine at Lanny's Alta Cucina in downtown. Salsa Limon, which makes its home base at Grand Plaza Mall, is among the city's popular food trucks that serve up tacos and other street food.

Upscale diners can send their taste buds around the world without ever leaving Fort Worth. Cuisine choices include Brazilian, Italian, German, and French, with dining experiences ranging from formal to fun. Ellerbe Fine Foods, in the Magnolia district, was named one of the Top 10 New Restaurants in America for 2010 by *Bon Appétit*.

But that's Fort Worth, a city that is completely at home in its own skin. Here is a place where you can savor the pleasures of great barbecue or boeuf bourguignon, a Tchaikovsky piano concerto or kick-up-your-heels two-step music. This bracing eclecticism engenders enormous civic pride. As Eric M. Lee said when he assumed directorship of the Kimbell Art Museum, "I'm proud to say that I am now a citizen of Fort Worth."

Above: Riscky's Barbeque, located in the Stockyards, is a Fort Worth institution. Opposite page, from left: Jamming at the Lone Star Nightclub; Reckless Kelly performs at Billy Bob's.

Above, from left: Indoor Rodeo at Will Rogers Equestrian Center; a ball game at Rangers Ballpark in Arlington.

COWBOY UP

From cowboys who rope and ride to Cowboys who run and tackle, Fort Worth is serious about its sports. Professional and college teams provide year-round spectator sports action. The region also boasts numerous parks and lakes, along with a highly regarded zoo and botanical garden, where families can enjoy Fort Worth from the outside.

As a Western city and the historic jumping-off place for the old Chisholm Trail, Fort Worth has proudly observed an annual rite since 1896: the Fort Worth Stock Show and Rodeo. One of the nation's premier events, it features bronc and bull riding, trick riders, mariachi music, museum exhibits, and the annual All Western Parade through downtown Cowtown. In 2012, some 1,200 rodeo athletes and 22,000 head of livestock provided entertainment for the 1.1 million visitors who came through the turnstiles.

Fort Worth is also the home range for the National Cutting Horse Association (NCHA) and the American Paint Horse Association (APHA). Founded in 1946, the NCHA produces national and world championships in the sport of cutting cows from the herd, while working to preserve the cutting horse's heritage as an indispensable working breed. The APHA's mission is to maintain pedigrees of American paint horses—perhaps the most emblematic of Western stock horses—through strict bloodlines and body type.

CHAPTERFOUR

41

Much of the city's equestrian activity takes place at the Will Rogers Equestrian Center, with its multiple arenas and up to 2,200 stalls accommodating the Fort Worth Stock Show and Rodeo, the Southwestern Exposition and Livestock Show, competitions for quarter horses and cutting horses, and world championships for paint horses and appaloosas.

Football fans only have to travel a few miles east to Arlington, where Cowboys Stadium is home to "America's Team." Owned and managed by Jerry Jones, the Dallas Cowboys are the highest-valued sports franchise in U.S. history, according to *Forbes*. Quarterback Tony Romo follows in the hallowed footsteps of Roger Staubach, who took the team to glory in the 1970s and 1980s. The team regained its swagger in the 1990s with Troy Aikman, Emmitt Smith, and Michael Irvin—a who's who of Hall of Famers.

The $1.5 billion stadium, which opened in 2009, is immense, with state-of-the-art amenities and a scoreboard seemingly as big as all of Texas. The stadium hosted the 2011 Super Bowl, not to mention the 2010 NBA All-Star Game, setting a Guinness World Record with the highest attendance for a basketball game with 108,713. Popular tours of the stadium provide access to everything from the playing field and postgame interviews room to the Cowboys locker room and press box.

For anyone who loves the spirit of collegiate athletics, Texas Christian University's sports programs include a powerhouse football team that boasts the historic accomplishments of players such as Heisman Trophy winner Davey O'Brien, Sammy Baugh, and LaDainian Tomlinson. Led by Coach Gary Patterson, the winningest coach in TCU history, the Horned Frogs have joined the elite ranks of college football. In 2011 the Frogs capped a perfect regular season with a Rose Bowl title, beating Wisconsin on New Year's Day.

The $164 million in improvements to Amon G. Carter Stadium, where the Horned Frogs play home games, ensures that the facility will be one of Texas' premier sports venues for years to come. The stadium is the site of the annual Bell Helicopter Armed Forces Bowl, a college bowl game that recognizes all five branches of the military.

This page: The annual Bell Helicopter Armed Forces Bowl, which featured a match-up between BYU and Tulsa in 2011, returned to TCU's newly renovated Amon G. Carter Stadium in 2012. Opposite page, from left: Dallas Cowboys quarterback Tony Romo in a game against the Chicago Bears; TCU fans cheer on the Horned Frogs.

This page: A pit stop during the NASCAR Sprint Cup Samsung 500 at Texas Motor Speedway. Opposite page: The Fort Worth Cats in action; the ninth green at the PGA's 2012 Crowne Plaza Invitational at Colonial golf tournament.

Not all the sports action in North Texas takes place on the gridiron. Rangers Ballpark in Arlington is a retro-style venue that harks back to the national pastime's golden era. After the 2010 season, the Rangers spent millions upgrading the audio and video systems, including installing a 5,000-square-foot, high-definition video board. In 2011, the team spent $12 million to build a two-story sports bar, indoor children's play area and new center field club. In 2012 work began on $12 million in upgrades, including the private club behind home plate. Behind-the-scenes-tours offer a glimpse of the dugout, clubhouse, and many other facets of this beautiful venue.

The Rangers date back to 1961, when they were formed as the Washington Senators. Since 1971, they have been making life tough for opponents in Arlington. The Rangers' rich pitching tradition is reflected in the stellar careers of past greats Ferguson Jenkins and Nolan Ryan, now the Rangers' CEO and president. More recently, led by Josh Hamilton and Nelson Cruz, the Rangers have become one of the most feared teams in the American League.

Fort Worth also boasts the minor-league Fort Worth Cats, who play in the North American Baseball League. Although not affiliated with the major leagues, the Cats have had some players who went on to stellar major league careers, including Dodger greats Duke Snider and Maury Wills. A game at LaGrave Field, located a few minutes north of the Upper West Side, offers all the thrills of the game in an intimate setting where fans can practically touch the players.

On the northern edge of Fort Worth, Texas Motor Speedway is home to the NASCAR Sprint Cup Series every April and November, along with the popular Camping World Truck Series for race-modified pickup trucks. The venue, which seats 159,585 ardent fans, also hosts IndyCar events and has a dirt track for dirt-racing enthusiasts.

The venerable Colonial Country Club is the showcase for the annual Crowne Plaza Invitational, the longest-running PGA event still being held at the original site (since 1946). The traditional tartan plaid jacket, which is bestowed on the winner, was draped on the shoulders of hometown favorite Ben Hogan five times.

Fort Worth Au Naturel

Fort Worth has numerous outdoor attractions, from a leading zoo and botanical garden to parks and lakes. Located just west of the Berkeley neighborhood outside downtown, the Fort Worth Zoo is one of the finest facilities in the nation, according to such publications as *Family Life, the Los Angeles Times, USA Today,* and *Southern Living*. The zoo's newest addition is a MOLA (Museum of Living Art), a 30,000-square-foot herpetarium that is home to some of the most exotic and endangered species on the planet, including 5,000

reptiles, amphibians, and more. The zoo also features such exhibits as the World of Primates, Meerkat Mounds, African Savannah, and Texas Wild!, complete with coyotes, jaguars, ocelots, and other species.

Established in 1934, the Fort Worth Botanical Garden is located just south of the Cultural District. This 109-acre zen oasis features about 2,500 species of exotic and native plants in more than 20 specialty gardens, from a rose garden to a xeriscape demonstrating water conservation.

The adjacent Botanical Research Institute of Texas (BRIT) is an international scientific research and learning center focused on botanical solutions to such global issues as sustainable food sources and pollution clean-up. This unique institute, which is open to the public, offers changing exhibits on and tours of the facility.

Connecting these and other Fort Worth attractions is Trinity River Trails, a 40-mile riverside system of walking, biking, hiking, and horseback trails. A project of the Trinity River Vision Plans, Trinity Rivers Trails feature picnic areas, a fishing pier, launch sites for kayaks and canoes, and more. The new Cowtown Wakepark, near Northside Drive, offers wakeboarding, a hybrid of surfing and waterskiing.

Native flora and fauna inhabit the Fort Worth Nature Center and Refuge, one of the largest city-owned nature centers in the United States. Comprised of woodlands, prairie, and wetlands, this hidden jewel features an interpretive center and more than 20 miles of hiking trails.

A 10-mile drive southwest of downtown, Benbrook Lake is one of Fort Worth's most popular recreation spots. The lake and surrounding land provide opportunities for a wealth of activities, including camping, picnicking, hunting, fishing, boating, and more.

Located on the west fork of the Trinity River, Lake Worth is a few minutes north of Fort Worth. Built in 1914 as a reservoir and for recreation, this is a favorite spot for fishing for largemouth bass, spotted bass, catfish, and white bass.

Eagle Mountain Lake is perfect for those who love boating. Eagle Mountain Marina features wet and dry slips, trailer storage, a stocked ship store, and a gas dock. In addition, fishing is very popular here, along with such water sports as water skiing, wakeboarding, and kayaking. There are also picnic areas, as well as trails and campgrounds.

On the shores of Eagle Mountain Lake is The Golf Club at the Resort, ranked one of the finest golf courses in North Texas. This championship-caliber layout is one of 20 courses located within the city. Rivercrest Country Club, Fort Worth's oldest country club, opened in 1911 and has hosted such legends as Ben Hogan, Byron Nelson, and Babe Didrikson Zaharias. The Mira Vista Country Club, designed by PGA golfer Tom Weiskopf, offers a park-line environment with native grasses and wildflowers.

From tee time on the links to kick-off at Cowboys Stadium, Fort Worth residents enjoy a year-round slate of spectator sports and recreation.

This page: A butterfly at the Fort Worth Botanical Garden; hitting a side rail at the Cowtown Wakepark on the banks of the Trinity River.
Opposite page: A photographer moves in for a close-up at the Fort Worth Zoo.

47

Above: Spanning the Trinity River in Fort Worth, the Phyllis J. Tiley Memorial Bridge is the first arch-supported stress-ribbon bridge in North America.

TRADITIONS AND INNOVATIONS

PART TWO

49

Above, from left: The Texas Christian University campus is a fortress of knowledge; the University of Texas at Arlington is home of the Mavericks.

Education

FORTRESS OF KNOWLEDGE

Living and learning in Fort Worth go hand in hand. From grade schoolers to adults committed to a life of continued education, area residents and students from other cities and states have myriad opportunities to attain valuable, enriching knowledge.

Education in the Fort Worth area includes outstanding public and private schools from preschool through grade 12. In addition to the three Rs, the city's public school systems are singled out in Sperling's Best Places for their excellent library and counseling services, boasting more of these resources per student than the national average. Among Fort Worth's many excellent private schools, the Fort Worth Academy of Fine Arts has earned a Gold national ranking on *U.S. News & World Report*'s Best High Schools survey.

Beyond senior year, colleges and universities in Fort Worth and the Metroplex area offer a wide variety of outstanding programs. Texas Christian University (TCU) has been touted by *U.S. News, Forbes*, and the Carnegie Commission, among others, as a top-tier university. Spread across a beautiful 325-acre campus, TCU constructed many of its buildings in the Beaux-Arts architecture of the surrounding area. TCU offers 118 undergraduate majors, 56 master's degree programs, and 21 doctoral programs, with outstanding business and journalism schools leading the way.

CHAPTERFIVE

TCU's journalism program was the first at a private university in Texas to be accredited by the Accrediting Council for Education in Journalism and Mass Communications. One of only 18 accredited programs at private universities in the United States, it boasts a full-time faculty with more than 250 collective years of field experience. The new Texas Center for Community Journalism, one of only five centers in the United States dedicated to supporting community journalism, provides workshops, seminars, and consulting services for community newspapers in Texas. The center will also help these publications to develop effective Web editions.

Renowned professors, innovative academics, and real-world experience helped TCU's Neeley School of Business soar to No. 56 from No. 69 in the 2013 *U.S. News & World Report* ranking of the Best Undergraduate Business Programs.

The Neeley Entrepreneurship Program was ranked No. 9 in the country by *Bloomberg Businessweek* and No. 25 on *The Princeton Review*'s list of Top Undergraduate Schools for Entrepreneurship in 2012.

With a student population nearing 35,000 strong, University of Texas at Arlington (UTA) could very well be its own city. One of Texas' premier universities, UTA boasts everything from the highly regarded School of Engineering and College of Business to the School of Urban and Public Affairs and the School of Architecture, the only such credited institution in North Texas.

The Carnegie Foundation has classified UTA as a High Research Activity institution, measured by such factors as research expenditures, number of research doctorates awarded, and number of research-focused faculty. The university's

NFL Hall of Fame lineman "Mean" Joe Greene, 1971 Miss America Phyllis George, and novelist Larry McMurtry all know the UNT alma mater.

Ten UNT programs were ranked in the top 100 nationally by the 2011 *U.S. News* study. City Management and Urban Policy, Clinical Psychology, and Library and Information Study are just a few programs that have garnered praise for UNT. There are 12 colleges and schools offering 97 bachelor's degree programs and 101 master's degree paths, plus 50 doctoral degree programs.

nationally ranked College of Engineering offers eight baccalaureate, 12 master's, and nine doctorate programs. The College of Nursing is generally considered one of the nation's finest, and the College of Business has an outstanding record for preparing students to pass the challenging Certified Public Accounting exam.

When they're not acing exams, the UTA Mavericks can take part in the university's 14 NCAA Division I varsity sports programs, including basketball, baseball, golf, volleyball, and track. In 2010–11, the men's basketball program set a school record for wins, including a 16-game win streak, powering them to the National Invitational Tournament. The women's basketball squad has made it to the NCAA Tournament several times.

From its first days in 1890 as a private teachers college to its current status as a public research institute with an annual operating budget of nearly $400 million, the University of North Texas (UNT) has grown into one of the region's most renowned academic institutions, with more than 35,000 students as of 2011. Located in Denton, north of Fort Worth, UNT boasts an alumni list that is a veritable who's who of Texas culture: Roy Orbison, Meat Loaf, Pat Boone,

This page, from left: The TCU Horned Frogs take on all comers at Amon G. Carter Stadium; this UTA Mavericks fan is ready to cheer on her team.
Opposite page: The campus of the University of North Texas.

The UNT Health Science Center, located in Fort Worth's Cultural District, prepares students for careers in health care through its School of Public Health, School of Health Professions, Texas College of Osteopathic Medicine, and UNT College of Pharmacy. The Graduate School of Biomedical Science is home to state-of-the-art research facilities where students work side by side with world-renowned faculty to solve some of today's challenging health issues.

No discussion of UNT would be complete without a note about the College of Music, located on the Denton campus. The largest music college in the nation accredited by the National Association of Schools of Music, it offers perform-ance, composition, education, theory, and jazz studies. The college's jazz

studies were ranked No. 1 on *U.S. News*' Annual Best Graduate Schools study every year the study was published up until the category was retired.

Business and education top the list of popular majors at Texas Wesleyan University, another outstanding Fort Worth institution. With 42 undergraduate majors, 13 graduate programs, and three doctoral programs, Wesleyan has the right choice for just about every student, with programs developed by the School of Education, the School of Arts & Letters, the School of Natural and Social Sciences, and other schools.

A number of specialty programs also draw students here, including the International Studies and the Study Abroad programs. The school's unique PreProfessional Program provides students with critical information to guide them to successful admission into graduate or professional programs, with strategies that include mentoring and networking with professionals in fields ranging from dentistry to ministry and counseling.

In 2013 the Texas Wesleyan University School of Law will become the Texas A&M School of Law at Texas Wesleyan University. The law school's externship program, 30-hour community-related pro bono requirement, law clinic, and other facets prepare students for the rigors of the legal field.

Since its establishment in 1908, Southwestern Baptist Theological Seminary has graduated nearly 50,000 students from every state and more than 50 countries, making this Southern Baptist Convention–associated seminary one of the largest in the world. Offering bachelor's degree programs, plus master's and doctoral degrees, Southwestern guides students through their choice of 18 tracks. Social work, corporate chaplaincy, and urban evangelism are just a few of the paths that students pursue here.

Six schools comprise Southwestern, including The School of Theology and The Roy Fish School of Evangelism and Missions. The School of Church Music is an exceptional training ground where students can choose from a number of master's degree programs and pursue a Ph.D. The school's Southwestern Master Chorale and Southwestern Singers perform nationally at high-profile venues including Lincoln Center in New York.

Graduate degrees in biblical counseling, children's ministry, and women's programs are offered by The Jack Terry School of Church and Family Ministries, with programs in preaching at The School of Theology. Southwestern reaches out with online theological education, as well as campuses throughout the state and region, and even as far away as Bonn, Germany. Journalist Bill Moyers and former Arkansas governor Mike Huckabee are just two of Southwestern's distinguished alums.

Less than an hour southwest of Fort Worth in Stephenville, Tarleton State University ranks among the most affordable four-year public universities. Part of the Texas A&M system, Tarleton has more than 12,000 students enrolled within two campuses, making it the second-largest university in the A&M system in terms of enrollment, behind only Texas A&M at College Station. Students at Tarleton's Southwest Metroplex Center in Fort Worth can choose from in-class, blended, or online courses.

Tarleton devotes resources to important fields such as the sciences. The $13 million science building at nearby Hunewell Ranch, built in 2008, includes a state-of-the-art planetarium and observatory with a research-grade telescope.

Tarleton's many colleges give students a wide range of options for study. The College of Agricultural and Environmental Sciences offers BS, MS, and other degrees in agricultural and consumer sciences and animal science and wildlife management, plus environmental and agricultural management. The Medical Laboratory Sciences (MLS) program is the only one of its kind in the Fort Worth area, offering a Master of Science in MLS with three areas of concentration: Molecular Diagnostics, Laboratory Management, and Cytogenetics.

Tarleton also has an outstanding music program, housed in the three-venue Clyde H. Wells Fine Arts Center. Stellar athletic programs include everything from football and baseball to men's and women's basketball, cross country, and track and field. The university competes at the NCAA Division II level. A 70,000-square-foot sports recreation center has weight rooms, racquetball courts, a track, and a gym, among other amenities.

Texas Woman's University (TWU) in Denton features an outstanding selection of majors and degrees in the sciences, arts, education, business, and other popular fields of endeavor. In 2011 *Forbes* ranked the university among the top 25 percent of colleges for undergraduates. TWU's occupational and physical therapy graduate programs were highly ranked by *U.S. News* in its 2012 survey. Through the university's online degree programs, through which

students can pursue knowledge in such fields as criminal justice, food systems administration, and management.

TWU is also recognized for its diversity. In 2012 *U.S. News* ranked it in the top three for the state and in the top 10 nationally among universities with the most diverse populations. *Hispanic Outlook in Higher Education* magazine and the Texas Higher Education Coordinating Board have recognized the university for its Hispanic enrollment and number of bachelor's and master's degrees awarded to Hispanics.

TWU competes at the Division II level in basketball, soccer, softball, volleyball, and other sports. The Pioneers' gymnastics squad has advanced to the USA Gymnastics Team Finals every year since 1992 and won nine titles.

Since its founding in 1965, Tarrant County College has grown from a student body of 4,440 students at its first campus to serving more than 100,000 students today. The college's five campuses include the new Trinity River Campus in downtown Fort Worth. TCC offers four types of degrees: Associate of Arts, Associate of Science, Associate of Arts in Teaching, and Associate of Applied Science. Certificates of completion are offered in 55 areas of study, along with a number of Continuing Education Program courses.

TCC provides a wide range of learning options, from certificates of completion and courses through Continuing Education, along with12 TCC learning centers across the country and the online Distance Learning Program. TCC programs transfer to colleges, universities, and the workplace, enabling students to create their own seamless path to the future.

Through its Achieving the Dream program, TCC helps to narrow student achievement gaps and create sustainable strategies for academic progress. Outreach programs at TCC also include everything from Early College High School for accelerated students to the Visions Unlimited Program, in which

the college teams with local homeless shelters to provide those in need with opportunities to learn.

The skilled workforce that TCC produces has helped to generate more than $844.7 million in regional income because of students' higher earnings and impact on business activity. And TCC's 3,240 faculty and staff pump $349 million annually into Tarrant County's economy.

Students looking for practical career training have several options in Fort worth. Remington College offers degrees and certificates in a broad range of fields, from nursing and dental hygiene to business administration and computer technology. Students with an artistic bent can acquire practical skills in Web design and other in-demand fields at The Art Institute of Fort Worth.

This rich amalgam of professional schools, community colleges, and four-year universities reflects Fort Worth's ongoing commitment to providing a rewarding, lifelong learning experience.

This page, from left: The Texas Woman's University soccer team in action; Tarrant County College student nurses receive training. Opposite page: Students stroll to class at Texas Woman's University.

57

Health Care

METROPLEX SUPERSTAR

The health care sector in the Metroplex accounted for 15 percent of the region's economic activity in 2011, or about $52 billion, and provided jobs for more than 30,000 people in the Fort Worth area. Facilities ranging from some of the state's top hospitals to dozens of specialty care centers offer more than 175 medical specialties. The Metroplex also supports a top life sciences cluster that keeps the beacon of research shining on this region.

Fort Worth's medical district is situated in the Near Southside, an eclectic area south of downtown. Complementing the five major health care systems are myriad clinics and the renowned University of North Texas Health Science Center, ranked as the nation's 35th-best medical school by *U.S. News & World Report* for 2013. Located adjacent to the Cultural District, the university comprises the Texas College of Osteopathic Medicine, the Graduate School of Biomedical Sciences, the School of Public Health, and the School of Health Professions.

Texas Health Harris Methodist Hospital Fort Worth, in the medical district, was ranked among the top 15 hospitals in Texas on *U.S. News & World Report*'s 2013 Best Hospitals list. The hospital is part of Texas Health Resources, the largest nonprofit, faith-based health care system in North Texas (in terms of patients served), which operates three acute-care hospitals in Fort Worth. The 726-bed Texas Health Fort Worth, a regional referral center, specializes in oncology, trauma, women's services, and cardiology, with a 100-bed heart center. The hospital was one of the first in the region to offer its atrial fibrillation patients Arctic Front Cardiac CryoAblation—a minimally invasive procedure delivering a coolant instead of heat, and significantly reducing the risk of damage to the tissue around the heart.

CHAPTERSIX

Texas Health Fort Worth is literally on the rise. In spring 2012, the hospital broke ground for a three-story, $57.7 million emergency care center that, at 75,000 square feet, will nearly triple the existing emergency department space when completed in fall 2013. The newest addition to Texas Health Resources, Texas Health Harris Methodist Hospital Alliance opened in September 2012.

In 2012 the 213-bed Huguley Memorial Medical Center, in Burleson, joined Texas Health Resources through a joint venture with Adventist Health System. The acute-care hospital includes two intensive-care units, a progressive-care unit, an open heart surgery center, a behavioral health center and a 24/7 emergency department. More than 350 primary care and specialty physicians provide a wide range of inpatient and outpatient services. Lone Star Orthopaedic and Spine Specialists, formerly located in the Huguley medical offices, plans to open

a free-standing clinic on the Huguley campus in March 2013 that will include an outpatient therapy center operated by medical center staff.

Huguley is on the forefront of technological advances. In 2012 HIMSS Analytics recognized Huguley for achieving Stage 6 on the Electronic Medical Record Adoption Model—one of only 6.2 percent of the more than 5,300 U.S. hospitals tracked that had reached Stage 6 as of April 1, 2012.

Another high achiever in the medical district is Baylor All Saints Medical Center, a 525-bed facility that is part of the extensive, Dallas-based Baylor Health Care System. Baylor All Saints ranks among the top 20 hospitals in Texas, according to *U.S. News & World Report*. Among its services is the Annette C. and Harold C. Simmons Transplant Institute, offering transplants

offices throughout north Texas. *U.S. News* ranked Children's as the 18th-best pediatric hospital in the nation for neonatology and among the top 40 for neurology and neurosurgery, diabetes and endocrinology, nephrology, cancer, and pulmonology.

Children's clinical research arm, which is an active partner in clinical trials with major companies such as Astra Zeneca, GlaxoSmithKline, and Medtronic, specializes in cystic fibrosis, neuroblastoma, and neurosciences. Neurology researchers, for example, are studying seizure reduction and freedom, improvement in motor function, and neuromodulation technology.

of the liver, kidney and pancreas, heart and lung, blood and marrow, islet cell, and small bowel. The Institute collaborates with Baylor University Medical Center, on the Dallas campus. The hospital itself, working hand in hand with the Baylor Research Institute in Dallas, coordinates and conducts clinical trials for all the hospitals and research centers in the system. Recent research applications have ranged from customizable cancer vaccines to an ultrasound-targeted microbubble transport system that delivers drugs or genes to specific tissues to rejuvenate the cells.

The headquarters of one of the nation's leading pediatric hospitals also can be found in the medical district: Cook Children's Health Care System, whose facilities include the 429-bed Medical Center (the core of the system), Northeast Hospital, a pediatric surgery center, and more than 60 primary care

This page: UNT Health Science Center's Medical Education and Training Building. Opposite page, from left: A surgical team performs a procedure at JPS;

In spring 2012, Children's completed most of a $250 million expansion when it opened the 283,000 square-foot Dodson Specialty Clinics (housing outpatient operating rooms and specialized services), the expanded neonatal intensive care unit, and a new indoor playground and food court.

John Peter Smith (JPS) dates back to 1877, when Smith, a future mayor of the city, deeded five acres for the city's first public hospital—yet its services today are comprehensive and leading-edge. The John Peter Smith (JPS) Health Network brings outstanding nephrology and pulmonary programs to the region, as well as excellent ear/nose/throat, neurology and neurosurgery, gynecology,

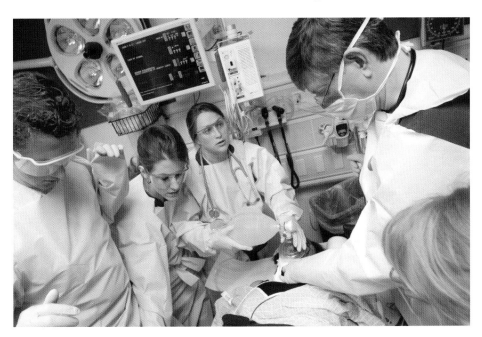

urology, and behavioral health care. Tarrant County's only Level I trauma center, JPS also offers an AIDS treatment center and two psychiatric facilities: Trinity Springs Pavilion for crisis stabilization and short-term treatment, and one of the nation's busiest psychiatric emergency centers. The main teaching hospital for the Texas College of Osteopathic Medicine at the University of North Texas Health Science Center, it also provides surgical residency programs for both the University of Texas Southwestern Medical Center and Baylor University Medical Center. In May 2007, JPS surgeons became the first in Fort Worth to use the da Vinci Surgical System robotic technology in the operating room.

Plans are under way for JPS to expand into the six-acre property across the street that housed the St. Joseph Hospital complex. Work begins in 2013 to clear the 10-building property over an anticipated three years. The vacant land will initially be converted to green space and feature an exercise course until expansion plans are finalized.

The 320-bed Plaza Medical Center of Fort Worth, affiliated with the UNT Health Science Center, rounds out the five major health care systems in the medical district. A referral center for Tarrant County as well as counties within a 90-mile radius, Plaza offers comprehensive services while focusing on three specialties: neurosciences, cardiac care, and orthopedics—and its accomplishments in these areas are significant. Through its technologically advanced Neuroscience Center, Plaza became the first hospital in Fort Worth to offer a dedicated stroke program, and its epileptic care unit was the first to provide round-the-clock adult EEG monitoring. Plaza cardiologists decreased the time from heart attack to treatment to 45 minutes (half of the national goal of 90 minutes), and they count among their standard tools the revolutionary Impella device (the world's tiniest

pump), which assists the heart in pumping blood during the intervention. At the Joint Center of Fort Worth at Plaza, orthopedic surgeons partner with colleagues from the Texas Hip and Knee Center to develop techniques to help osteoarthritis patients resume active lives. Innovations include hip resurfacing, which preserves more of the original bone structure by adding a cobalt chrome implant to the hip area, and a high-performance alternative to total knee replacement utilizing a resurfacing implant to preserve bone and ligament that typically would be sacrificed.

A member hospital in the educational consortium Texas Osteopathic Postdoctoral Training Institutions (Texas OPTI), Plaza offers residencies and

fellowships to medical school graduates who would benefit from the guidance of skilled professionals. In 2012 the hospital was in the final stages of a $90 million, multiyear expansion that is updating its intensive care unit and pharmacy and adding operating rooms.

The Moncrief Cancer Institute is another world-class institute in the medical district. An affiliate of the UT Southwestern Harold C. Simmons Comprehensive Cancer Center, this community-based cancer prevention and support center collaborates with agencies in the area to make sure patients have access to every resource available. That includes the 13 major clinical care programs offered at the Simmons center and a National Cancer Institute–designated cancer center, as well as research generated by the UT Southwestern Medical Center, whose faculty includes five Nobel Prize winners.

Health care facilities aren't limited to the medical district—they abound throughout the Metroplex. UNT Health Science Center maintains 45 clinics throughout Tarrant County, with nearly 220 physicians providing care in a wide range of specialties.

Several renowned hospitals in Fort Worth dedicate themselves to long-term care and rehabilitation. The 67-bed Kindred Hospital downtown is part of

Kentucky-based Kindred Healthcare network of 89 hospitals in 28 states. Through aggressive, specialized, interdisciplinary care, Kindred hospitals discharged an average of nearly 70 percent of their patients in 2011 to a lower level of care after a stay of 28 days.

Fort Worth today is capitalizing on efforts that have extended over more than a century to create a health care and research hub envied throughout the nation. With world-renowned universities, leading hospitals, and a collaborative culture, the health care sector in Fort Worth is helping to redefine the landscape of human health.

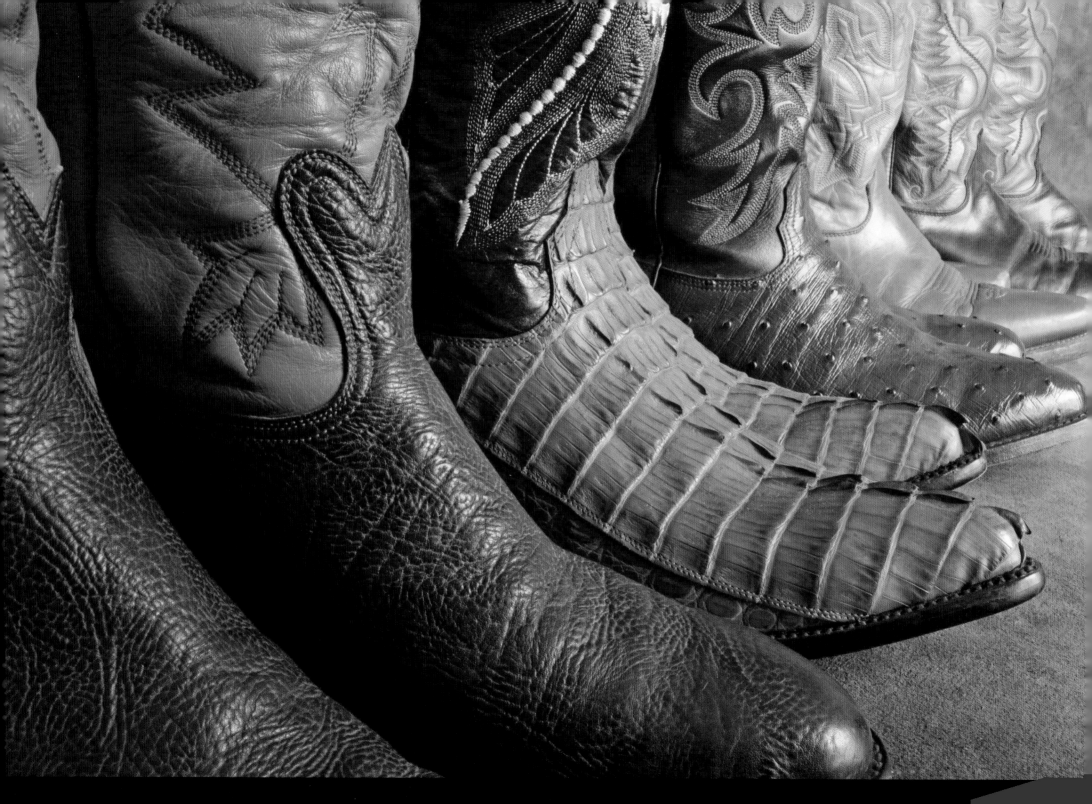

FORT WORTH WARES

Fort Worth has built an impressive roster of international companies whose products are known worldwide. The ready access to transportation, availability of turnkey industrial space, and abundance of business incentives have lured companies with marquee names such as General Electric and Dannon Yogurt to the Fort Worth area. Manufacturing concerns based in Fort Worth turn out everything from salsa and beer to aircraft and locomotives, pharmaceuticals and electronics to packaging and apparel.

Cowtown is Chow Town

Much of Fort Worth's cuisine is influenced by Mexico and the Deep South—hot peppers and chow chow relish, for instance—but the city is also justly famous for a surprisingly diverse range of food products, including yogurt.

Best Maid Products Inc. got into the food game as a family business in 1926, with grocer Jesse Otis Dalton selling the homemade pies and mayonnaise that his wife, Mildred, whipped up. In 1962, the company acquired Del-Dixi Products, whose pickles remain one of the strongest sellers in Texas, and in 2010, Best Maid became the official pickle of the NFL Dallas Cowboys. Best Maid today makes pickles, jalapeños, relish, and dressings.

CHAPTER**SEVEN**

Renfro Foods has been making condiments in Fort Worth since 1940, first with its Dixieland line of syrups and then chow-chow, a sweet and sour relish of (usually) cabbage, onion, and green tomato. Renfro acquired the Mexican recipes of Olé Foods in 1972, and today it makes and markets Mrs. Renfro's gourmet salsas, relishes, syrups, and sauces.

Fort Worth has plenty of ice-cold cervezas to wash down those hot peppers. The Miller brewery in Fort Worth, which MillerCoors bought in 1966, was the first of the company's plants to brew Miller Lite. The facility pumps out nine million barrels of suds a year on the site of the former Carling Brewing Company.

Rahr & Sons Brewing Co., founded in 2004, has won 15 nationally recognized awards for its brews, including a Bronze Medal at the 2008 World Beer Cup for Bucking Bock and 2009 National Grand Champion from the U.S. Beer Tasting Championships for Iron Thistle.

Yogurt seems an unlikely pairing with the hearty fare of Fort Worth, but Dannon Yogurt, which was founded in Spain in 1919, opened its Fort Worth plant in 1979 as part of its westward expansion. A subsidiary of Groupe Danone, now headquartered in Paris, Danone has decentralized its world operations to produce Dannon, Stonyfield Farm, and Activia; Evian bottled water; and baby

Made in Fort Worth

Fort Worth is the proud site of numerous vehicle manufacturing and design concerns, running the gamut from military aircraft to locomotives. The roster of successful military aircraft that have been produced by Lockheed Martin Aeronautics Co., headquartered in Fort Worth, includes the F-16 Fighting Falcon, the C-130J jumbo transport, and the F-117 Nighthawk stealth attack aircraft. The company's current operations are focused on the F-35 Lightning II multiple-role fighter, while its "Go Green" environmental initiative stresses the need to reduce carbon emissions, landfill waste, and water usage.

foods, particularly in China and Latin America. Because dairy necessarily involves intensive use of environmental resources, Danone has put itself on the road to reducing its carbon footprint from 2008 to 2012 by 30 percent—and reached a reduction of 27.5 percent by 2011.

O.B. Macaroni Co. has been making noodles in Fort Worth since 1899. Its products include Q&Q brand fideo—a pasta line for the Hispanic market—as well as pastas and egg noodles under the O.B. brand. The company also encourages private label, institutional, and government orders.

Bimbo Bakeries USA, the largest baker in the country, may not be a household name, but its brands are. They include Oroweat, Thomas', and Entenmann's. They also include Mrs. Baird's, which was the country's largest family-owned bakery when Grupo Bimbo acquired it in 1998 and made Fort Worth the center of Bimbo's U.S. operations. Mindful of its environmental impact, Bimbo has introduced hybrid trucks in Oregon and Denver and has implemented programs to reduce its energy use and waste output.

Above, from left: A Bimbo Bakery truck delivers fresh bread; Dannon Yogurt is among the healthy food products made in Fort Worth. Opposite page: The UK took delivery of this F-35 Lightning II jet built at Lockheed Martin in Fort Worth.

Fort Worth–based Bell Helicopter also builds and designs helicopters and tiltrotor aircraft, such as the V-22 Osprey, a joint production with Boeing that combines the speed and range of a turboprop airplane with the vertical takeoff and landing (VTOL) capabilities of a helicopter. Bell also builds the UH-1Y Yankee—descended from the iconic "Huey" of the Vietnam War—and the AH-1Z Zulu attack helicopter, along with helicopters for police and commercial use.

Commercial aircraft products also have found a home in Fort Worth. RECARO Aircraft Seating Americas, part of a German conglomerate, manufactures aircraft seats for American Airlines, Delta, and other international clientele at its 100-square-foot facility at AllianceTexas. Fort Worth is one of three manufacturing locations for ThyssenKrupp Airport Systems, which produces passenger boarding bridges and systems used at airports around the world.

In 2011 General Electric announced an investment of more than $190 million to open a pair of factories in Fort Worth. One plant will build motorized wheels for heavy-duty mining trucks, while the other will build locomotives, including GE's fuel-efficient Evolution series. Located near the Alliance Global Logistics Hub, the $96 million, 900,000-square-foot locomotive plant is on track to generate 500 jobs upon opening in 2012, with another 275 jobs down the line.

General Motors invested $530 million in the expansion of its assembly plant in nearby Arlington for a new line of sport utility vehicles that will go into production in the second half of 2013. The combined body shop and sheet metal parts stamping facility is adding approximately 425,000 square feet to the 3.7-million-square-foot complex.

A Good Bill of Health

Fort Worth's life sciences industry is enjoying a good bill of health. This thriving sector includes 450 biomedical companies and more than 1,000 research and development and testing laboratories.

The eyes of Texas are on Alcon, perhaps best known for its contact lens products. Founded in Fort Worth in 1945, the company is now owned by Novartis, but its main corporate offices are still here, along with two major manufacturing facilities and its primary R&D site, the 650,000-square-foot William C. Conner Research Center. With nearly 3,200 employees, it is one of the region's largest employers, producing ophthalmic surgical equipment in addition to personal eye-care products.

Galderma Laboratories, which got started as a joint venture between Nestlé and L'Oréal in 1981, focuses solely on treatments for dermatological disorders, producing such well-known skin-care products as the Cetaphil line of moisturizers. Nestlé acquired Alcon in 1977, which led to Galderma's assumption of Alcon's dermatology business in 1988.

Privately owned Ferris Mfg. Corp., which makes and distributes bandages and diaper rash products, is investing $5.5 million in capital expenditures in a new Fort Worth headquarters and a manufacturing and distribution center. The Texas Enterprise Fund (TEF), which has invested some $439.8 million in projects that have attracted $14.7 billion in investments and created some 59,000 jobs since it was created in 2003, is ponying up another $450,000.

Hard-Wired for Success

The Hinckley-Tandy Leather Company, founded in Fort Worth in 1919, shed its leather business in 1954 and changed its name to Tandy Corporation in 1959. Four years later, the company expanded into electronics when it acquired RadioShack, a Boston company. Tandy took on the RadioShack moniker in 2000 and today is a Fortune 500 company based in Fort Worth.

Mucinex, a popular over-the-counter expectorant, was developed in Fort Worth by Adams Respiratory Therapeutics. Alvaro F. Guillem, Adams' vice president and general manager, is now president and CEO of ZS Pharma, Inc. Founded in 2008, the Fort Worth company is focused on the development and commercialization of oral sorbent technology. The research team developed a compound known as zirconium silicate (ZrSi), which selectively removes life-threatening toxins in patients suffering from kidney and liver disease and related conditions.

RadioShack offers trade-ins for electronic devices once they've outlived their usefulness. In fact, computer manufacturers are required to offer free and convenient recycling of their equipment in Texas. Fort Worth provides three drop-off points for recycling outmoded laptops, modems, servers, and other e-waste. Companies such as STS Electronic Recycling offer free recycling as well.

Further expanding Fort Worth's biopharmaceutical bootprint is Healthpoint Biotherapeutics, which opened an 80,000-square-foot research operation in Fort Worth in 2006. Healthpoint focuses on developing and commercializing bioactive therapies for skin repair and regeneration, with a portfolio that includes wound cleansers, gel dressings, and surgical scrubs. In June 2012, the company announced a 25,000-square-foot upgrade to its facilities, anticipating 51 new hires and an investment of $60 million.

Q-Edge, a subsidiary of FoxConn Electronics, makes components for computers, cell phones, and other consumer electronics. Its facility at the Alliance complex is expected to create up to 500 jobs and generate an economic impact of more than $700 million in the region.

GameStop Corp., a Fortune 500 company and the largest seller of video game hardware and software, relocated to a larger facility in Grapevine in Tarrant County. The company, which employees nearly 3,000 people in North Texas, received $1.25 million in tax incentives from the city of Grapevine to relocate there.

It's all in the Packaging

Fort Worth produces attractive, high-quality packaging for both people and products.

Pratt Industries, the fifth-largest box manufacturer in the United States and the world's largest, privately held paper and packaging company, plans to add 140 new jobs to Fort Worth's manufacturing sector by the end of 2013. Its $25 million, nearly 329,000-square-foot facility at RiverPark 700 produces corrugated boards from 100 percent recycled materials.

From the rodeo circuit to the assembly line, hard work calls for sturdy work clothes. Williamson-Dickie Manufacturing Co., based in Fort Worth, is a leader in the production of work apparel, Its Dickies brand features apparel and footwear, as well as school uniforms and medical scrubs. Justin Brands, which moved to Fort Worth in 1925 and is now a Berkshire Hathaway company, makes cowboy boots, along with work, safety, and sports footwear.

In a tradition begun by Amon G. Carter, Sr., publisher of the *Fort Worth Star-Telegram*, the Shady Oaks Western hat made by Peters Bros. Hats has been given to nine U.S. presidents since 1923. Though he rarely wore hats, President Kennedy was presented with a custom-made Shady Oaks hat at the Fort Worth Chamber of Commerce breakfast on November 22, 1963, prior to his departure to Dallas. That hat has never been found, but Peters Bros. Hats still makes the Shady Oaks one at a time, by hand.

This emblematic brand reflects Fort Worth's roots as a Western cowtown; the dozens of other manufacturers that have located here since have helped to blaze a trail of growth and prosperity for the region.

Above, from left: Fort Worth's transportation and distribution needs are served by a wide range of providers, including this FedEx Express jet and BNSF locomotive.

FROM POINT A TO POINT B

Fort Worth's importance as a transportation center dates back to its days as a jumping-off point for the Chisholm Trail, when cattlemen would stop in town to pick up supplies for the long drive north to the Kansas railheads. Today the city is located within 48 highway hours or four air hours of all major markets in North America. Three interstates and two international airports now serve the area, along with a pair of Class I railroads.

The arrival of the Texas and Pacific Railway in 1876 didn't end the importance of the cattle trails, but it did make Fort Worth the westernmost railhead for the cattle industry, breathing new life into a city hit hard by Reconstruction. The Union Pacific Railroad (UP) and the BNSF Railway provide major rail service in Fort Worth today.

In terms of dollars and environmental costs, rail remains the most efficient method for moving freight on land. A train can take a ton of cargo for a 500-mile ride on a gallon of diesel and can haul 300 truckloads of freight.

CHAPTER EIGHT

Traffic improvements for the city include the Chisholm Trail Parkway, a 27.6-mile toll road stretching southwest between downtown Fort Worth and the suburb of Cleburne in Johnson County. The multijurisdictional project, whose partners include the North Texas Tollway Authority (NTTA), the Texas Department of Transportation (TxDOT), and Tarrant and Johnson counties, is scheduled to open in 2014. The NTTA, TxDOT, and the City of Fort Worth worked closely with a citizens advisory group to steer the landscaping of the six-lane section between I-30 through the southwestern part of the city.

Headquartered in Fort Worth, BNSF provides daily intermodal service at the Alliance Global Logistics Hub. Union Pacific also maintains a presence in the region. Its Davidson hump yard, one of its larger classification facilities, is a critical connector for moving freight between Southern California, the East Coast, and Mexico. Both companies are helping to fund the Tower 55 Multimodal Project to relieve rail congestion south of the I-30/35W interchange, where 10 passenger and freight routes converge.

Fort Worth lies on the trucking corridors connecting Mexico with the Great Lakes and the Gulf ports with Southern California. I-30 and I-35W cross in downtown Fort Worth, while I-20 passes through the city south of downtown. I-820 horseshoes northward to form a beltway around the city.

This page: A Union Pacific freight car. Opposite page, from left: A trucker heads back to his rig at a rest stop; the Texas Department of Transportation TransVision Center monitors traffic on North Texas roads.

Air Supply

Cross-country air travelers are familiar with Dallas/Fort Worth International Airport, which ranks fourth in the world for operations and eighth for passengers served—nearly 647,000 operations and 57.8 million passengers in 2011, including 5.5 million international travelers. Nonstop service from DFW reached 144 U.S. cities and 50 international destinations as of June 2012—including the Cayman Islands—with six carriers and 12 international destinations added in the preceding year and a half. DFW recently introduced CLEAR, a biometric

screening service, at Terminal E, allowing members to confirm their identity and pass through security with the touch of a fingertip.

DFW is the largest connecting hub for American Airlines, as well as its corporate home. American is the airport's dominant carrier, with American Airlines or American Eagle operating out of four of the airport's five terminals.

The airport launched a multibillion-dollar, seven-year revitalization project in 2011. The Terminal Renewal and Improvement Program (TRIP) is improving parking, expanding security checkpoints, and bringing more than 30 new concessions to Terminal A beginning in 2013. Led by Freese and Nichols, a Fort Worth consulting firm, the project will include new commuter rail stations for the Fort Worth Transportation Authority and Dallas Rapid Transit.

The airport is also an important cargo handler, with a full range of logistics support, three million square feet of freight facilities, and round-the-clock customs clearance. DFW employs a variety of environmentally sustainable practices designed to promote recycling, reuse, and waste reduction, and uses zero-emissions vehicles.

Other airports in the region include Meacham International Airport, five miles north of downtown, and Spinks Airport in southeast Fort Worth, a general-aviation reliever airport. Fort Worth Alliance Airport (AFW), an industrial airport serving the Alliance Global Logistics Hub, is a major inland port, featuring a large intermodal yard and proximity to I-35W.

Fort Worth's intermodal facilities have attracted such companies as FedEx, whose Southwest Regional Sort Hub is found at Alliance, and transport and logistics group LinkAmerica. Citing Fort Worth's importance as a logistics hub, Oklahoma-based LinkAmerica announced plans in 2012 for a 24,000-square-foot corporate office and training center in CentrePort Business Park, which will house its executive offices and should bring 140 jobs to the area. LinkAmerica is also attracted to Fort Worth's talent pool, whose readiness ranges from driving to administration to senior management.

The "T"

Like any Western U.S. city, Fort Worth has grown accustomed to the convenience of the personal automobile, but the city has taken measures to augment its streets and freeways with an integrated system of bike routes, commuter rail, buses, and vanpools to connect people to jobs, attractions, and transportation hubs.

The Fort Worth Transportation Authority, or The T, is a regional transportation authority serving Tarrant County and north-central Texas. It owns the Trinity

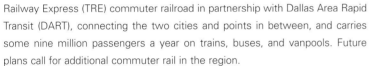

Railway Express (TRE) commuter railroad in partnership with Dallas Area Rapid Transit (DART), connecting the two cities and points in between, and carries some nine million passengers a year on trains, buses, and vanpools. Future plans call for additional commuter rail in the region.

TRE's CentrePort/DFW Airport Station is convenient to Dallas Mavericks/Dallas Stars games as well as DFW via shuttle, while the Intermodal Transportation Center (ITC) in downtown Fort Worth is a hub for local and long-distance ground transport. The T also provides a Safari Shuttle between the ITC and the Fort Worth Zoo on Saturdays from May to October. To ease air pollution—and take advantage of a local natural resource—The T's buses, vans, and trolleys are primarily fueled by compressed natural gas.

Bike! Fort Worth

One of the most enjoyable ways to get around Fort Worth is also fueled by an abundant natural resource—people power. Bike! Fort Worth, the city's bicycle transportation plan, promotes bike safety and hopes to triple the number of two-wheeling commuters. Fort Worth already has numerous on-street bike lanes, off-street bike paths, and bus/bike routes in place, with many more in the planning stage. Bicycling in Fort Worth has also been given an official and personal nod from Mayor Betsy Price, who promotes and cycles with Tour de Fort Worth on her weekly rides around town, kids' rides, and charity rides.

Whether by air or rail, bike or bus, Fort Worth residents and businesses enjoy an unrivaled transportation system.

This page, from left: An all-electric vehicle is demonstrated in the Centreport/DFW TRE station parking lot on Clean Air Action Day; a TRE locomotive.
Opposite page: Biking along the West Fork of the Trinity River.

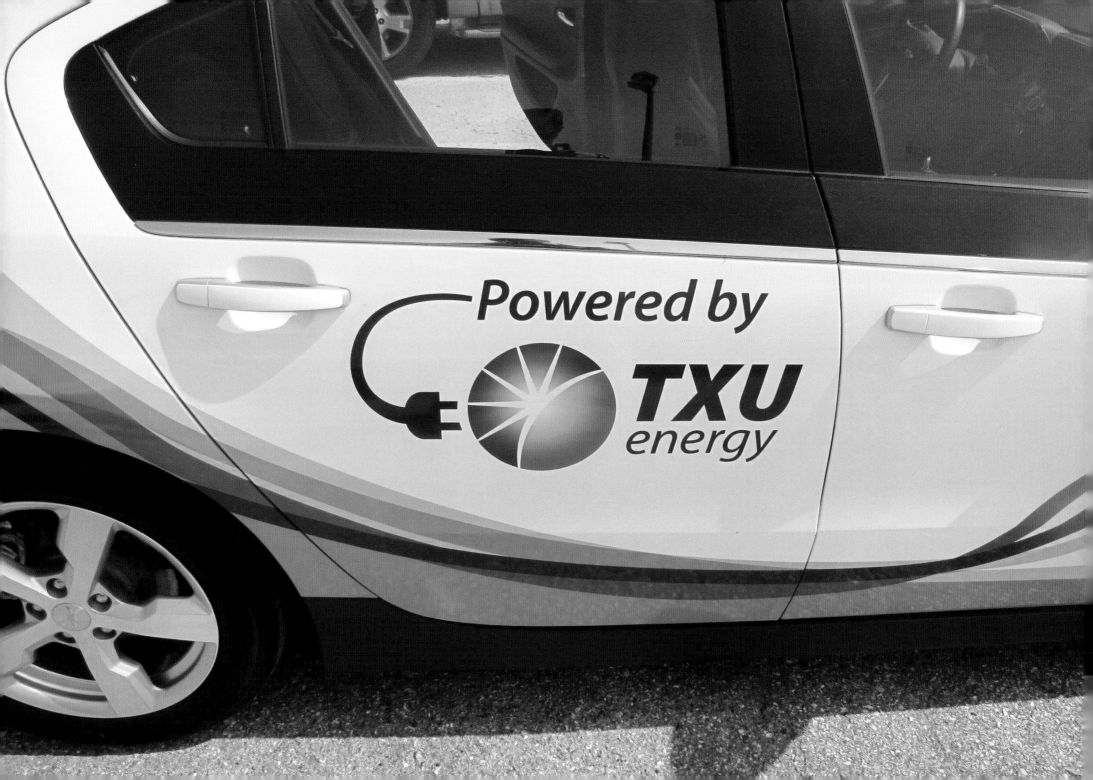

FUELED FOR THE FUTURE

From the oil boom era to the present, Fort Worth has been an important energy producer in north-central Texas. In addition to supporting a modern energy infrastructure, Fort Worth sits atop the 5,000-square-mile Barnett Shale gas field, estimated to contain from 40 to 55 trillion cubic feet of natural gas. The reserves, which lie some 1.5 miles below the surface, have only recently become available for extraction through hydraulic fracturing.

Companies both large and small are seeking ways to tap into this clean-burning domestic energy while minimizing pollution and damage to the environment. The operations hub for the Barnett Shale, Chesapeake Energy is the first company to ever drill for and extract natural gas from beneath a major metropolitan airport—Dallas/Fort Worth International. Chesapeake Energy conducts its operations from the regional corporate office, which resides in an award-winning, 20-story building overlooking the Trinity River.

CHAPTERNINE

In 2010 XTO Energy of Fort Worth was purchased by Exxon, making the combined company the largest natural gas producer in the U.S. Using the newest technology, XTO draws on the combined expertise of both companies to produce affordable, reliable, clean-burning natural gas in the United States and abroad. Another Fort Worth–based natural gas and oil exploration and production company, Quicksilver Resources Inc. has leased approximately 140,000 net acres of the Barnett Shale field.

Launched in 2002 by two brothers from Cisco, Texas, FTS International is a leading independent provider of well stimulation services for the U.S. oil and gas industry. Exploration and production companies use FTS' services to enhance their recovery rates from wells drilled in shale and other unconventional reservoirs.

Natural gas utility Atmos Energy serves about 3 million customers in a nine-state region between the Appalachians and the Rockies. The company also operates a large intrastate pipeline in Texas, one of the country's largest, and markets natural gas supplies to industrial customers and municipalities in 22 states. The company's headquarters are in Dallas.

Of course, natural gas is not the only energy source in the region. TXU Energy, the state's top electricity provider, first saw light as a consolidation of 13 electric companies in 1912, though it indirectly traces its ancestry back to 1882. A private equity buyout of TXU Corp. in 2007 made TXU Energy the retail electricity provider, Oncor the transmission and distribution utility, and Luminant the wholesale electricity generation provider. Keeping up with the times, TXU Energy fired up a mobile Web site and iPhone app in 2011.

Houston-based Reliant Energy supplies electricity to 1.5 million residences, businesses, manufacturers, and government entities in Texas. Reliant makes

moving to Fort Worth easy not only for energy customers, but serves as a one-stop shop for phone, cable, and Internet service as well. Its green energy plans include a solar leasing program and 100 percent wind-energy power generation.

Retail electric providers such as Ambit Energy Texas can now purchase energy at wholesales prices and sell it at reduced cost to consumers. Ambit offers environmentally friendly electricity plans certified by the Green-e Energy program.

This page, from left: TXU power lines bring electricity to the Metroplex area; propane gas provides another source of energy for consumers.
Opposite page: This natural gas rig is tapping into the Barnett Shale natural gas field.

This page: The Herbarium at the Botanical Research Institute of Texas (BRIT). Opposite page: BRIT's Living Roof; Green Mountain Energy solar panels at the Fort Worth Zoo.

Going Green

Fort Worth is faced with an enormous challenge: to provide energy for a growing population while increasing energy efficiency and creating a sustainable environment. Among the local organizations addressing this issue is the Botanical Research Institute of Texas (BRIT). The BRIT headquarters, which is adjacent to the Fort Worth Botanical Garden, was designed to reduce energy and water consumption, enhance indoor environmental quality, and use recyclable and renewable materials. The facility's living roof is itself a laboratory where researchers from BRIT, local universities, and the community can conduct in-depth data collection and research on the roof's long-term effects on energy consumption and the urban heat island. BRIT researchers are also working in the United States and Peru on sustainable agriculture projects.

The City of Fort Worth is also actively engaged in sustainability efforts. As a partner in the Better Buildings Challenge, a Department of Energy (DOE) national leadership program focused on encouraging greater energy efficiency, Fort Worth has pledged to reduce energy use in 5.7 million square feet of its public facilities by 20 percent by 2020, and to work with other city building owners to achieve similar savings.

"The City of Fort Worth is pleased to join the Better Buildings Challenge, helping lead the nation to greater energy efficiency, economic growth, and a cleaner environment," said Tom Higgins, Fort Worth City Manager.

By capitalizing on clean energy resources and pursuing energy conservation measures, Fort Worth is on the path to creating a sustainable future for the city and its citizens.

PARTNERS IN PROGRESS
Profiles of Leading Fort Worth Companies and Organizations

PARTTHREE

PROFILES OF COMPANIES AND ORGANIZATIONS
Aerospace

Bell Helicopter

Bell Helicopter is on a mission to change the way the world flies with superior vertical lift solutions that save lives, preserve freedom, and provide customers exceptional value. Each day the company's three business segments—military aircraft, commercial aircraft, and customer support and services—operate in numerous markets, including military, emergency medical services, oil and gas, parapublic, and corporate transportation.

This page, left: With the speed of a turboprop plane and the hovering maneuverability and agility of a helicopter, the Bell-Boeing V-22 Osprey is a true multi-mission aircraft. Whether the job is transporting troops, delivering cargo, or flying Special Forces operations, the V-22 brings more capabilities to the mission than any other aircraft. Right: The Bell 429 delivers exceptional speed, capacity, and flexibility. Its cabin is exceptionally spacious, with seating for up to eight passengers, and it can be reconfigured for any number of different missions.

Bell Helicopter, a Textron Company, employs more than 11,000 employees, from test pilots, engineers, and highly skilled maintenance and repair experts to assemblers and sales and marketing specialists. The company's diverse workforce of talented men and women is a point of differentiation in the aviation industry.

The company's global headquarters, located in Fort Worth, Texas, is being revitalized to provide employees with better, more comfortable work environments. Bell Helicopter also maintains specialized assembly facilities in Amarillo, Texas, and Mirabel, Canada.

As international demand has increased, the company's global footprint has grown into an ever-expanding network of strategically located sales, logistics, supply, and service centers in key locations in Europe, Canada, the United States,

and Asia. In 2012 alone, Bell Helicopter opened a new world-class service facility in Singapore and upgraded facilities in India and Prague; it also signed an agreement for the first flight-training school in China. Now Bell Helicopter plans to move further into European and Asian markets, grow its foreign military sales, and continue expanding its commercial aircraft segment with innovative new products and upgrades.

Founded in July 1935 by Lawrence D. Bell, and known as Bell Aircraft Corporation, Bell Helicopter specialized in the design and production of fighter aircraft, including the first American jet fighter, the Bell XP-59. The Bell X-1 was also produced, and it broke the sound barrier in 1947. In 1941, just before the United States entered World War II, the first Bell helicopter was built. It took its first flight in December 1942. In the years since, Bell Helicopter has delivered more than 35,000 helicopters to customers in 120 countries around the globe.

The company's military aircraft have served the United States Army, Navy, Marines, and Air Force. With more than 150,000 flight hours, the Bell-Boeing V-22 Osprey has proven to be one of the safest and most cost-effective military aircraft platforms. The Osprey's groundbreaking tiltrotor technology, pioneered by Bell Helicopter, lifts like a helicopter and flies like an airplane, with twice the speed, three times the payload, and five times the range of traditional helicopters. Bell Helicopter also supplies the United States military with the OH-58D "Kiowa Warrior," the premier Army scout helicopter; the AH-1Z "Zulu," a highly advanced attack helicopter; and the UH-1Y "Yankee."

Bell Helicopter's commercial aircraft deliver reliable performance to customers, completing their vital missions—whether in oil and gas, helicopter emergency medical services, law enforcement, or corporate transportation. Two of Bell Helicopter's newest aircraft are the Bell 429 and the Bell 407GX. The Bell 429 offers an especially spacious cabin, with seating for up to eight passengers, and exceptional speed and flexibility. The Bell 407GX features the superior and recognized performance of the Bell 407 platform, with a state-of-the-art Garmin G1000H™ flight deck that provides critical flight information at a glance for greater situational awareness and safety.

Bell Helicopter's latest commercial design, the Bell 525 Relentless, is innovation at its best: it will be first in its class to incorporate breakthrough technology, including the new ARC Horizon flight deck and fly-by-wire flight controls. The Bell 525 Relentless combines an advanced aerodynamic design, a Next Generation GE® engine, and a rugged airframe to deliver best-in-class payload-range capability.

It's no surprise that Bell Helicopter's Customer Support and Services has been named number one for 18 consecutive years by *Professional Pilot* magazine and seven consecutive years by *Aviation International News*. The business segment offers the industry's most comprehensive customer support program, with services ranging from technologically advanced customization, aircraft refurbishment, and accessory options to unparalleled maintenance, repair and overhaul solutions, and personalized service offerings. Bell Helicopter's unsurpassed support network includes more than 120 customer service facilities in 34 countries, conveniently located supply centers, dozens of customer service representatives available 24/7, and dedicated product support engineers, all focused on fulfilling customer requirements, upholding global responsiveness, and lowering direct operating costs.

With five commercial platforms in production and one game-changing product in the design phase, Bell Helicopter's future is bright. The Bell 525 Relentless program is well underway and highly anticipated in numerous markets. With research and development at the core of its business strategy, Bell Helicopter is continuously improving design, test, and manufacturing capabilities; inspiring new ideas; and rapidly bringing innovative solutions to its customers.

For more information, please visit www.bellhelicopter.com.

This page, left: At Heli-Expo 2012 in Dallas, Bell Helicopter formally launched the Bell 525 "Relentless" Super-Medium Twin, the largest civil helicopter in the company's history. Ideal for a variety of missions, the 18,000-pound-plus helicopter will have a range of more than 400 nautical miles, a speed near 150 knots, and a ceiling of 20,000 feet. Right: The Bell Helicopter Training Academy, certified by the FAA, offers a complete line of training for Bell aircraft. Training programs blend theoretical knowledge instruction with specific aircraft training tasks conducted in advanced flight training devices such as the Bell 429 simulator as well as in the aircraft.

PROFILES OF COMPANIES AND ORGANIZATIONS
Cultural District

Fort Worth Museum of Science and History

Dedicated to lifelong learning and anchored by its rich collections, the Fort Worth Museum of Science and History engages this diverse community through creative, vibrant programs and exhibits interpreting science and the stories of Texas and the Southwest. Although its name, location, size, and scope have changed dramatically since 1941, the museum still serves a similar purpose: to provide an extraordinary educational environment.

This page: Located in the Fort Worth Cultural District, the Fort Worth Museum of Science and History offers innovative learning studios, interactive exhibits, an all-digital Noble Planetarium, and the Omni Theater, the biggest IMAX dome in the Southwest.

About the Museum

The Fort Worth Museum of Science and History is home to more than 175,000 historical and scientific objects. The science collection consists of many thousands of catalogued specimens that represent the disciplines of botany, entomology, malacology, ornithology, mineralogy, herpetology, mammalogy, invertebrate zoology, meteoritics, and paleontology. The herbarium collection of native plants from Texas and the United States dates from the late 1800s to the present. The museum is involved in ongoing regional paleontological digs for dinosaur fossils and has rich specimens from the Fort Worth region, including five new species of dinosaurs. The history collection encompasses a worldwide scope, ranging from prehistoric artifacts to items from many cultures from the late 1800s to the present, including pre-Columbian ceramic figures from Central America. The museum also houses a scientific teaching collection of 20,000 items that duplicate specimens in the permanent collection. These items are used for hands-on activities and are loaned to local schools and teachers. The history teaching collection has 2,400 pieces that are made available through school loan kits, with items ranging from cowboy gear to pioneer artifacts.

Museum School

For more than 60 years, the Fort Worth Museum of Science and History's Museum School program has been the foundation of the museum's work in early childhood learning. Since its founding in 1949, more than 200,000 children have participated in this one-of-a-kind program, which was the first in the United States to be accredited by the National Association for the Education of Young Children. The purpose of the Museum School is to give very young children—ages three to sixth grade—a chance to expand their mental horizons by helping them learn from vivid firsthand experiences about the wonderful and fascinating world of science around them.

Fort Worth Children's Museum

The Fort Worth Children's Museum harkens back to the 1941 Fort Worth Museum of Science and History's humble beginnings in a house on Summit Street. This Children's Museum gallery targets the museum's youngest guests—from birth to age eight—and those who care for them. The purpose is to encourage children to play because at this age, children learn through playing. The Children's Museum is a healthy kid's clinic, an infant/toddler developmental space, and a parent resource room that also serves as a multipurpose space that includes a family restroom, nursing room for mothers, and natural science space.

Omni IMAX Theater

Since its opening in April 1983, the Omni IMAX Theater has earned a reputation as one of the most engaging learning environments in the community. For more than

25 years, more than 10 million guests have journeyed to remote islands of the Pacific, explored deep under the ocean surface, splashed down the mighty Colorado of the Grand Canyon, stampeded across the vast Serengeti, traveled through the galaxy to the craters of Mars, and inched up the treacherous peaks of Mount Everest—all while never leaving North Texas.

Energy Blast

Energy Blast tells the dynamic story of energy resources in North Texas through a unique combination of science and history, bringing physics, technology, and innovative thinking to life as guests are asked to explore geophysical formations, calculate drilling depths and directions, and experiment with new resources. Guests of Energy Blast first enter through a multisensory prehistoric undersea environment similar to Fort Worth 300 million years ago into the

4-D theater, where they embark on a six-minute journey that tells the story of how natural gas formed within shale deposits of North Texas.

Noble Planetarium

The 90-seat Noble Planetarium brings the first Zeiss-manufactured hybrid planetarium system—an immersive all-dome video combined with a fiber-optic dual-hemisphere star projector to see more than 7,000 stars—to the Southwest United States. For more information, visit www.fortworthmuseum.org.

This page, clockwise from top left: In addition to its impressive all-dome video and fiber-optic dual-hemisphere star projector, the Noble Planetarium also features an exhibit area that provides large screens with up-to-the-minute views of the Sun, as well as downlinks offering the latest information from the Hubble Telescope. On exhibit at the museum, the state dinosaur of Texas, the *Paluxysaurus jonesi*, is estimated to have measured 70 feet long and 12 feet high at the shoulder, and weighed as much as 20 tons. A young patron of the Fort Worth Children's Museum learns through playing at one of the interactive exhibits.

Amon Carter Museum of American Art

A Fort Worth institution for more than 50 years, the Amon Carter Museum of American Art is among the foremost museums of American art in the United States. The museum was founded in 1961, fulfilling the dream of Fort Worth publisher and philanthropist Amon G. Carter (1879–1955) of establishing a museum free and open to the public.

Above: The Amon Carter Museum of American Art offers a diverse array of exhibitions, publications, and programs that help visitors of all ages and backgrounds connect to their shared cultural heritage through masterworks of American art. Admission to the museum is always free.

When the Amon Carter Museum of American Art opened, the collection consisted of a stellar body of works by the artists Frederic Remington and Charles M. Russell, known for their paintings and sculpture of the American West. Over the years, the museum's collection expanded dramatically, and today the Amon Carter houses more than 200,000 objects. The collection consists of paintings and sculpture by a range of American artists, including Alexander Calder, Frederic Church, Stuart Davis, Arthur Dove, Thomas Eakins, Winslow Homer, and Georgia O'Keeffe.

In addition to paintings and sculpture, the Amon Carter's holdings also include works on paper, rare books, and 45,000 exhibition-quality photographs, making the museum one of the country's major repositories of American photography.

The museum is also recognized as a national architectural treasure. Designed by Philip Johnson (1906–2005), the building is composed of teak, Arabian granite, and bronze wedded with the creamy, intricately patterned surface of native Texas shellstone. When Johnson was again engaged to design the museum's 2001 expansion, he declared the project "*the* building of my career."

Admission to the Amon Carter remains free to all, and more than 100,000 people visit each year. Adults, families, educators, and students from the community, around the state, and across the country connect to the collection each year through exhibitions and the extensive programs and resources offered at the museum. The range of free programs, always posted on the calendar on the

museum's website, include lecture series, tours for new parents, gallery and artist talks, family fun days, and crafting workshops. Along with treats and beverages, the Museum Store + Café offers a host of products related to American art. Free tours featuring highlights from the permanent collection take place every Thursday through Sunday at 2 p.m. and begin at the Information Desk.

The Amon Carter Museum of American Art is located within walking distance of four other world-class museums in the relaxing, park-like setting of Fort Worth's Cultural District, which is just west of downtown. The Amon Carter is open six days a week, features numerous exhibitions each year, and is always free. Visit www.cartermuseum.org to learn more.

Kimbell Art Museum

In its short history of 40 years, the Kimbell Art Museum has come to occupy a distinctive place in the international community of art museums. The Kimbell Art Foundation, which owns and operates the museum, was established in the 1930s by Kay and Velma Kimbell and Kay's sister and her husband, Dr. and Mrs. Coleman Carter.

This page, from left to right: The north portico and reflecting pool are just two examples of the Kimbell Art Museum's stunning design, created by architect Louis I. Kahn. This digital rendering depicts the south facade of the museum's new building, designed by renowned architect Renzo Piano.

The Kimbell Art Foundation originally collected mostly British and French portraits from the 18th and 19th centuries. When Mr. Kimbell died in 1964, the foundation set about building a museum using the personal fortunes of Mr. Kimbell and his wife, Velma.

By 1966 the foundation's board of directors had appointed the museum's first director and set the policy of forming "collections of the highest aesthetic quality, derived from any and all periods in man's history, and in any medium or style." Two aspects of that plan would have the greatest impact on changing the Kimbell collection: an expansion of vision to encompass world history and a new focus on a small number of key objects. Today the collection consists of about 350 works that touch individual high points of aesthetic beauty and historical importance.

The Kimbell's collections range in period from antiquity to the 20th century and include European masterpieces by artists such as Fra Angelico, Michelangelo, Caravaggio, Poussin, Velázquez, Monet, Picasso, and Matisse; important collections of Egyptian and classical antiquities; and Asian, Mesoamerican, and African art. The museum does not collect American art, nor works created after 1950, in order to more effectively complement the offerings of its neighbors: the Amon Carter Museum of American Art and the Modern Art Museum of Fort Worth.

Equally important in the development of the Kimbell as a major world museum has been its initiation of highly acclaimed international loan exhibitions, including retrospectives devoted to the great painters Poussin, Ribera, Tiepolo, Stubbs, Vigée Le Brun, Gauguin, and Monet. Other major exhibitions originated or co-organized by the Kimbell include *Spanish Still Life in the Golden Age, 1600–1650* (1985), *The Blood of Kings: A New Interpretation of Maya Art* (1986), *Loves of the Gods: Mythological Painting from Watteau to David* (1992), *Picturing the Bible: The Earliest Christian Art* (2007), and *Caravaggio and His Followers in Rome* (2011). The museum has also played host to major traveling exhibitions, beginning in 1973

with *Impressionist and Post-Impressionist Paintings from the U.S.S.R.* and including *The Great Bronze Age of China* (1980), *Impressionist Masterpieces from the Barnes Collection* (1994), *Hatshepsut: From Queen to Pharaoh* (2006), *The Impressionists: Master Paintings from the Art Institute of Chicago* (2008), and *Fiery Pool: The Maya and the Mythic Sea* (2010).

The Kimbell Art Museum, designed by the American architect Louis I. Kahn (1901–1974), is widely regarded as one of the outstanding architectural achievements of the modern era. A new building, designed by the renowned Italian architect Renzo Piano, is scheduled to open in 2013 and will provide space for special exhibitions, allowing the Kahn building to showcase the permanent collection. The new building will also provide the classrooms and studios that are essential to a full-scale museum education department, as well as a 294-seat auditorium, an expanded library, and generous underground parking.

Complimentary Acoustiguide audio tours are available for the permanent collection and building. More than 100 random-access stops feature the Kimbell's signature paintings and sculptures as well as Louis Kahn's architectural masterpiece. About 25 family-friendly stops are designed for children ages 7 to 12.

A full schedule of public programs relates the study and interpretation of the museum's collections and exhibitions to the needs and interests of diverse audiences. Regularly held programs include free symposia, lectures, gallery talks, and films; a book discussion group; activities for individuals with Alzheimer's;

tours for adults, students, and families; teacher training programs; university events; and a range of studio-art workshops and festivals for participants of all ages.

Many visitors enjoy homemade soups, salads, sandwiches, quiche, and dessert in the relaxing and beautiful ambience of the museum's Buffet Restaurant. Friday evenings feature a light dinner buffet of soups, salads, pasta dishes, and a vegetable torte, with a selection of wines and other beverages.

The Museum Shop offers an exceptional array of merchandise and the most extensive selection of art and architecture books in Fort Worth.

Admission to view the permanent collection is always free. For additional information about the Kimbell Art Museum, visit www.kimbellart.org.

This page, from left to right: Gustave Caillebotte's Impressionist oil-on-canvas painting, *On the Pont de l'Europe* (1876–77), uses cool tones to reflect Paris's stone, iron, and concrete construction. Michelangelo Buonarroti's *The Torment of Saint Anthony* (circa 1487–88), executed in tempera and oil on a wood panel, is Michelangelo's earliest known painting.

PROFILES OF COMPANIES AND ORGANIZATIONS
Economic Development/Business Organizations

Fort Worth Chamber of Commerce

In Fort Worth's Old West days, "partner" referred to rock-solid character, trustworthiness, and loyalty. That's how the Fort Worth business community has viewed the Fort Worth Chamber of Commerce since its founding in 1882.

The Chamber's 130-year partnership with the business community has created world-class economic engines, cultural centers, and quality of life. There's far more potential to be tapped as Fort Worth, the United States' 16th-largest city, creates new and better reasons for residents to live, work, and play here.

Much of the Chamber's work involves sensitive planning, presentations, and negotiating out of the public eye. Whether engaged in competitive economic development efforts, foreign trade missions, or marshaling support for a community need, the Chamber knows how to work with discretion. That's why it is known as the business community's custodian of projects that can take years of work. For example, the Chamber invested decades of involvement in major infrastructure initiatives such as the Chisholm Trail Parkway, scheduled for completion in 2014.

But there also is high-profile involvement. In 2007, the Chamber led a $593.6 million school bond campaign that won approval for the Fort Worth Independent School District's "Building the Vision" Capital Improvement Program that was completed in 2011 on time and under budget.

Meanwhile, the Chamber's Vision Fort Worth program invites residents ages 20 to 40 to help create a branding strategy to attract and retain talented young people. Participants earn their place in a time-tested partnership: the public-private sectors and the Chamber—an alliance that's rock-solid, trustworthy, and loyal to Fort Worth.

Visit www.fortworthchamber.com for more information about current Fort Worth Chamber projects.

PROFILES OF COMPANIES AND ORGANIZATIONS
Financial Institutions

Cash America International, Inc.

Serving America's under-banked population, Cash America International, Inc. (NYSE: CSH) helps people obtain funds for life's unexpected expenses. Based in Fort Worth, Cash America offers simple, accessible financial resources to its customers.

simple and fast. The company is committed to providing excellent customer service in a clean, brightly lit, professional setting.

With almost 500 employees at the corporate headquarters in downtown Fort Worth and more than 250 employees at stores in Fort Worth, Cash America has a strong presence in the community. Cash America employs nearly 6,000 people across the United States.

"I believe all organizations have a responsibility to contribute positively to the quality of life in their community," says Dan Feehan, Cash America President and CEO. "Cash America and the City of Fort Worth have a long-standing bond of cooperation that allows our company the opportunity to make a difference in the lives of our citizens through contributions of time, energy, intellectual capital, and money. Investing in our community is one of the most fulfilling investments we ever make."

Cash America's History

In 1983 Cash America founder Jack Daugherty opened the first Cash America Pawn in Irving, Texas, with the hope of building a company that would serve the under-banked population—those who could not get financial help from traditional financial lenders.

In 1987 the company made history by becoming the first chain of pawnshops to go public, currently trading under the ticker symbol "CSH" on the New York Stock Exchange. Cash America has expanded to become one of the largest pawnshop chains in the country.

Cash America purchased majority ownership in Prenda Fácil, which operates pawnshops in central and southern Mexico, in 2008.

Today the Cash America family of brands offers a multitude of financial services to help people in need, including collateralized loans, cash advances, pre-paid debit cards, auto equity loans, and more.

This page:
Cash America
International, Inc.'s
corporate headquarters
is located in
Fort Worth, Texas.

Cash America International, Inc. is the largest provider of secured, non-recourse loans, commonly referred to as pawn loans, in 23 states with more than 800 locations under the brand names Cash America Pawn, SuperPawn, Payday Advance, and Cashland. The company achieved a major milestone in 2008 by earning $1 billion in revenue.

Cash America prides itself on its skilled, friendly employees who treat customers with respect, explain in great detail the conditions of the loan, and make the transactions

Looking to the Future

Cash America has redefined the pawn industry with everything from modern store concepts and layouts to a comprehensive database for appraising collateral.

In October 2011, Cash America opened a new concept store, featuring innovative designs and new technologies unlike any other in the pawnshop industry. The store features hardwood floors and stained concrete as new remodeling upgrades and an innovative redesign to improve traffic flow and customer service experiences. The setup, designed to resemble small retail shops, features a jewelry department with wall cases separate from other merchandise.

Retail check-out counters are now separate from loan counters, offering more customer privacy for borrowers and improved service for all customers. The new design improves customer traffic flow during busy times and makes shopping easier for customers.

"The new concept store revolutionizes the image and reputation of pawnshops," says President of Retail Services Dennis Weese. "Cash America has always been a leader in the pawn industry, but the versatility of the new concept store takes us to the next level. It allows customers to find products quickly, helps them get in and out faster, and improves the overall customer experience."

Leading in Innovation

Innovative technology is a key component for companies to stay ahead in today's ever-changing marketplace. To that end, Cash America made it possible for customers in 32 states and several foreign countries to arrange consumer loans via the Internet by submitting an online application through Enova International, Inc., a wholly owned subsidiary of Cash America. The publication *Built in Chicago* named Enova one of its Top 100 Digital Companies in Chicago.

Since its acquisition by Cash America in 2006, Enova has become a leading provider of online financial services that is focused on customer service. Enova offers short-term consumer loans over the Internet. Enova offers products to people in the United States, the United Kingdom, Australia, and Canada.

Enova consistently introduces new products to meet the needs of customers today. In 2012 Enova began offering a longer-term loan to customers through NetCredit.com. Other services such as lines of credit and installment loans allow customers additional access to credit to cover an unexpected cost like medical bills or car or home repairs.

Lending a Hand

The Cash America team believes in connecting with the community and is committed to the neighborhoods and people it serves. Nationally, Cash America focuses its fund-raising efforts on the Juvenile Diabetes Research Foundation (JDRF) and Susan G. Komen for the Cure®.

Cash America is constantly looking for opportunities to support organizations that provide programs or support for education/financial literacy, public safety initiatives, families in need, natural disaster relief programs, and military and their families. It supports various organizations through volunteerism, donations, and resources.

This page, all photos: Cash America's new concept store, located at 3740 Altamesa Boulevard in Fort Worth, is leading the way for the pawnshop industry, with innovative designs and new technologies.

Southwest Bank

As the largest locally owned, independent commercial bank in Tarrant County, Southwest Bank is big enough to offer the stability and services of a national institution, but small enough to know every customer.

chief executive officer (CEO). Prior to forming First Texas BHC, Bryant served the North Texas community for many years as president and CEO of TexasBank, a successful community bank based in Weatherford, Texas. After TexasBank was sold, Bryant left the company to return to community banking, and formed First Texas BHC soon after.

The Local Business That Supports Local Businesses

The secret to Southwest Bank's success is a focus on community. Southwest Bank is owned and managed right in Fort Worth. This means that its people understand the unique needs of North Texas businesses and can quickly respond to customers and make decisions.

Southwest Bank truly reflects the culture and diversity of North Texas. The bank is inherently community-focused and relationship-driven, from its leaders, who are all active in local nonprofit organizations, to its Web site, which features the familiar faces of actual employees. Each year Southwest Bank and its employees give back to the community by supporting programs and volunteering time to help individuals and families in need. Every August employees donate school supplies to support the students at Westcreek Elementary School in the Fort Worth Independent School District. Every December employees collect toys for the Marine Corps' Toys for Tots program. Throughout the year, the bank and its employees support various community organizations, including the March of Dimes, Habitat for Humanity, and United Way of Tarrant County.

Fort Worth is a strong business community, and Southwest Bank is very involved in it. A top tier member of the Fort Worth Chamber of Commerce, the bank is a

The Bank That Knows Texas

Southwest Bank has served the people and businesses of North Texas for 50 years, fostering a culture of excellence, investing in the latest technology, and building lasting relationships. Founded in 1963, this Fort Worth–based community business has banking centers throughout North Texas. Today Southwest Bank is the largest locally owned, independent commercial bank in Tarrant County, offering strength, stability, and a strong track record of managing risk and delivering results.

In 2007 Southwest Bank was purchased by First Texas BHC, Inc. Made up of more than 400 local shareholders, this new holding company was led by long-time banker Vernon Bryant, Jr., who served as the company's founder, chairman, and

Above: Richard Barajas (center), Southwest Bank executive vice president and chief credit officer, is shown with Fort Worth–area banking center presidents (left to right) Jim Luttrell (Hulen), Brett Burns (Saginaw), Lori Baldock (Midtown), and Alec Barry (West 7th Street).

frequent sponsor of chamber events. In 2008 Bryant served as chairman of the Chamber Board. Southwest Bank also supports other civic organizations, as well as local arts and educational programs.

Bryant explains, "Community banks are directly invested in local families and local businesses—we all work together to build a better neighborhood. That's why community banking is here to stay."

The People Who Make It Happen

Southwest Bank understands that people—not processes—ultimately run a business, and with that in mind, only the best are hired. The leadership and management team has a combined 300-plus years of banking experience,

and its members are often recognized as outstanding professionals in their field. *Fort Worth, Texas* magazine named Bryant one of the 50 Most Powerful People in Town in 2007, and in 2009 he was selected as Fort Worth's Business Executive of the Year. Many of the bank's officers have been recognized as "40 Under 40" leaders by the *Fort Worth Business Press*, which spotlights not only professional achievement but also community leadership.

"Southwest Bank is built on an incredible team," Bryant says. "They truly care about our customers—their neighbors. I credit the company's success to their integrity and experience."

Southwest Bank Advantage

This community bank is also robust enough to offer services that compete against much larger institutions. Customers who take advantage of Southwest Bank's personal and business banking products have access to the latest online and mobile banking technology, as well as a wide range of treasury management, mortgage, investment, and wealth management services. Southwest Bank's Small Business Association lending program is consistently ranked as one of the top 10 programs in North Texas.

"North Texas is like no other place in the world," Bryant reflects, "And we set out to create an institution specifically suited to this community. We are genuinely committed to helping Fort Worth businesses grow. When local businesses succeed, we all benefit."

For more information, visit www.SouthwestBank.com.

This page: Convenient to customers who live and work near downtown Fort Worth and located near the vibrant Cultural District, the Southwest Bank West 7th Street banking center is one of many locations in the Tarrant County area.

Bank of Texas

Bank of Texas strives to offer the best in nationally competitive products and personalized service. This, combined with access to experienced bankers who work to truly understand each customer's personal and business financial needs, helps build proactive, successful partnerships.

As part of BOK Financial, a $26 billion financial services company, Bank of Texas is an integral division within a more than 100-year-old organization and the 21st-largest United States-based publicly traded bank holding company. As a testament to the company's strength, it was the largest commercial bank in the United States not to take Troubled Asset Relief Plan (TARP) funds. The bank experienced record earnings in 2010 and again in 2011.

Bank of Texas has been a part of the community for more than 15 years and its philosophy for doing business is simple: Local bankers providing local leadership and expertise to help and support local companies and individuals. The commitment to this philosophy is built on the understanding that banking is a relationship business.

Banking professionals at Bank of Texas work with clients in a variety of industries and offer a wide range of services, including commercial banking, wealth management, and mortgage and consumer banking. Mobile and online banking capabilities are also available to bank customers. Bank of Texas also offers specialized financial solutions to several niche industries. For example, it has groups focused on health care banking, commercial real estate banking, and energy banking. The parent company has been a leader in energy banking for more than a century.

Furthermore, because professionals at Bank of Texas are local, they can successfully help clients navigate the local financial landscape. Being a part of a larger organization, they can also deliver insights into national and international financial market trends and cycles, including the local, state, and federal regulatory environment. Bank of Texas also prides itself on its commitment to the greater Fort Worth community through philanthropic giving and employee volunteerism.

Bank of Texas is a local bank with a proven record of commitment to serving its clients. While many banks have struggled in recent years, Bank of Texas has remained financially sound. That is due to a corporate culture based on strategic, conservative growth and the highest level of integrity.

Moreover, Bank of Texas works hard to be a client's bank of choice and strives every day to be a reliable, reputable, and responsible corporate citizen. For additional information about Bank of Texas, please call 817-348-5748 or visit www.bankoftexas.com.

PROFILES OF COMPANIES AND ORGANIZATIONS
Health Care Services

Cook Children's Health Care System

Cook Children's Health Care System is one of the country's leading integrated pediatric health care organizations. This award-winning, not-for-profit system provides seamless health care exclusively for children through its eight entities: a medical center, physician network, home-health company, Northeast Hospital, pediatric surgery center, health plan, health services, and health foundation.

Based in Fort Worth, Texas, Cook Children's Health Care System has significant reach, with more than 60 primary and specialty care offices and clinics throughout North Texas. Its primary service region includes Denton, Hood, Johnson, Parker, Tarrant, and Wise counties, with an additional referral area encompassing more than half the state. However, patients and their families often travel great distances, from other states and countries, to make Cook Children's their destination for the best possible pediatric care. Cook Children's records approximately one million patient encounters each year through its hospitals, specialty clinics, neighborhood clinics, physician offices, outpatient settings, and home-health company.

Cook Children's heritage dates back to 1918, and throughout the decades since, it has been a leader in pediatric health care by fostering continual change and robust growth, while always embracing its abiding promise "to improve the health of every child in its region through the prevention and treatment of illness, disease, and injury." And that promise is one that more than 5,000 Cook Children's employees commit to keeping every day.

Cook Children's lives up to its pledge by combining the art of caring with strong, integrity-led collaboration. Cook Children's also is proud to lead clinical research and utilize the best available technology, all while re-investing hundreds of millions of dollars into programs that benefit the community.

Expanding to Serve

Cook Children's promise is not just for the children who need health care now; it is also for the children of the future. In 2009 Cook Children's Medical Center began the largest campus expansion in its history, a 40 percent increase, to meet the needs of a growing community for generations to come.

One of the expansion's highlights is an all-private room Neonatal Intensive Care Unit (NICU), the largest such unit in the nation. It features 99 rooms and 106 beds, with special accommodations for twins, triplets, and quadruplets. The state-of-the-art

unit features specialized equipment and monitoring, allowing Cook Children's staff to provide the highest level of care for preemies and infants that need critical care.

Also part of the expansion was the construction of the Dodson Specialty Clinics building, which houses 18 specialties under one roof for the convenience of Cook Children's patient families.

This page: Cook Children's Medical Center offers a state-of-the-art Neonatal Intensive Care Unit (NICU) with 99 private rooms. This private-room setting is specifically designed so parents can comfortably stay with their babies around-the-clock, while infants receive the highest level of care.

Some of these specialty clinics include:

- **The Jane and John Justin Neurosciences Center,** which offers one of the largest, most technologically advanced pediatric neurosciences programs in the country. Its highly skilled doctors and staff are dedicated to recognizing and treating diseases, disorders, and injuries of developing brains, spinal cords, nerves, and muscles.
- **The Hematology and Oncology Center,** which works to cure children and teenagers with cancer and blood-related disorders through innovative research and treatment advances. Thanks to the expansion, Cook Children's is one of only a few centers in the nation to offer a high-dose radiation therapy known as metaiodobenzylguanidine (MIBG) to treat neuroblastoma.
- **The Heart Center,** which provides comprehensive care for neonates, infants, and children with acquired or congenital heart and cardiovascular defects. The team includes cardiologists, cardiothoracic surgeons, cardiac anesthesiologists, a cardiac intensivist, perfusionists, and nurse specialists.

Benefiting the Community

In addition to growing its medical center services, Cook Children's constantly expands its reach to help improve the health of all children in the region, specifically those that are underserved. The organization works diligently with more than 150 partner organizations to improve the safety and health of at-risk children through education, disease and injury prevention, and support. Cook Children's operates five neighborhood clinics so that children in underserved areas can have access to primary medical care. In fiscal year 2011, Cook Children's provided more than $93 million in total community benefits.

Rick W. Merrill, president and CEO of Cook Children's Health Care System, notes, "Because we are a not-for-profit organization, we can focus on providing exceptional care, rather than improving the bottom line. This enables us to make a real difference for the children and families we serve. And it is why we continue to grow and expand services both at our medical center and out in the community to meet the needs of our patients and their families. This is in keeping with our promise to improve the health of every child in our region and our commitment to making our community the healthiest place to raise a child."

To learn more about the life-changing services provided by Cook Children's Health Care System, visit the organization's Web site at www.cookchildrens.org.

This page, left: Cook Children's is committed to providing one-stop health care services for its pediatric patients. Its extraordinary team of physicians, clinicians, caregivers, and professionals share an unwavering commitment to providing family- and patient-centered care. This page, right: Cook Children's collaborates with more than 150 community partners throughout North Texas to assess and address children's health needs.

Baylor All Saints Medical Center at Fort Worth

From preventive medicine to advanced treatment methods for fighting disease, this long-time Fort Worth health care provider strives to provide exemplary care for the community at every opportunity, focusing on patient care, education, research, and community service.

Neuroscience Center

In 2001 Baylor Fort Worth opened the Laura Leonard Hallum Neuroscience Center, which offers advances such as deep brain stimulation, neck and spine surgical services, including skull base surgery, and a certified stroke program.

Expanded Resources

In 2002 All Saints Hospitals formed an affiliation with the Baylor Health Care System (BHCS), a not-for-profit, faith-based network of hospitals, primary care centers, rehabilitation clinics, senior health centers, affiliated ambulatory surgery centers, and the Baylor Research Institute. With the affiliation, the hospital was renamed Baylor All Saints Medical Center at Fort Worth. The affiliation also brought access to the resources of BHCS. One result is a partnership of Annette C. and Harold C. Simmons Transplant Institute with Baylor All Saints Medical Center at Fort Worth, which opened an inpatient transplant unit. Expansion at Baylor Fort Worth includes the Paul and Judy Andrews Women's Hospital, which opened in 2008.

Today Baylor Fort Worth and Baylor Fort Worth's Andrews Women's Hospital continue to excel in all health care services, including cancer care, neuroscience care, transplantation, rehabilitation, heart and vascular care, women's services, and more. They are committed to providing quality health care that makes a difference in the lives of people in Greater Fort Worth.

For more information, visit www.baylorhealth.com/AllSaints.

Since its founding in 1906, Baylor All Saints Medical Center at Fort Worth has provided advanced health care to its community. Located near downtown Fort Worth, the Center began as All Saints Episcopal Hospital, which cared for the sick on the Texas frontier. It grew steadily during the first half of the century, becoming a progressive health center devoted to quality medical care, public health education, research, and community service.

Over the decades, Baylor Fort Worth continued to offer leading-edge health care and opened specialized medical centers such as the Moncrief Cancer Center, the Moncrief Ambulatory Care Center, and the Carter Rehabilitation and Fitness Center.

Above: The exterior of Baylor All Saints Medical Center at Fort Worth.

PROFILES OF COMPANIES AND ORGANIZATIONS

Higher Education

Tarleton State University

With innovative new programs, Tarleton State University addresses the needs of today's students as they prepare to take their place in the modern workforce. At Tarleton, the belief that its students deserve the highest quality education and boundless opportunities is at the heart of all its programs. Tarleton provides a caring community ready to join with students on their road to achievement and success.

Tarleton State University, a member of The Texas A&M University System, extended its reach to the Dallas–Fort Worth Metroplex in 1978. The university, founded in 1899 in Stephenville, Texas, saw the growing demand for laboratory professionals in the field of medicine and today is the only program of its kind in the Dallas–Fort Worth Metroplex. The demand for affordable education options in the Metroplex grew, and in 2007 Tarleton State University opened the Southwest Metroplex Center in the Hickman Building on Camp Bowie Boulevard. Degree options expanded to include graduate and undergraduate programs in business, psychology, criminal justice, and education. Enrollment rapidly grew to 675 students, and in 2012 the student population exceeded 1,200 students.

Tarleton understands not everyone is looking for the traditional college experience. Family and work responsibilities take the place of student activities and campus

life. The Southwest Metroplex Center in Fort Worth provides adult learners in the Dallas–Fort Worth Metroplex an opportunity to continue their education in a manner that fits their lifestyle. Fort Worth Texans are serious students in need of degree options that fit in their budget and schedule. Tarleton ranks among the most affordable public four-year universities in Texas and is in the top 25 percent for affordability of tuition and related costs. Classes are offered days, nights, weekends, and online to accommodate the diverse student body. By combining quality education with real world experience, Tarleton gives graduates a jump start to a successful future. The safe campus and small student-to-teacher ratio support a diverse learning environment, ideal for student success.

A variety of degree options, including nontraditional degrees, enable students to reach their educational and professional goals. The Southwest Metroplex Center's undergraduate programs are bachelor's degree completion programs, designed to build on associate level degrees earned at Tarrant County College and other surrounding community colleges. Nontraditional bachelor's degrees allow students to apply military and technical training and/or work experience to 36 hours of elective coursework. These include degrees in business, manufacturing and industrial technology, information technology, and criminal justice.

The master's degree programs offered at the Southwest Metroplex Center are courses taught by highly credentialed faculty, many of whom have professional experience from local corporations.

Tarleton's Medical Laboratory Science programs have continued to expand in Fort Worth since 1978. Recognizing the need for Allied Health Professionals to complete a bachelor's degree, Tarleton now offers the Bachelor's of Applied Technology (BAT) in Health Professions Technology. The BAT builds upon associate programs such as emergency medical technician (EMT), dental hygiene, respiratory care, and other terminal health care degrees. Obtaining a BAT aides in promotion to leadership positions in the respective fields. The Medical Laboratory Sciences (MLS) program

has also expanded graduate program offerings, with the cutting-edge Master of Science in MLS with three concentration areas: Molecular Diagnostics, Laboratory Management, and Cytogenetics.

Tarleton's nationally recognized education programs, both undergraduate and graduate, are some of the most successful programs in Fort Worth. The Bachelor of Interdisciplinary Studies program offers three certification options and is taught in a cohort model in which students work together to learn and graduate as one unit. Graduate programs in Curriculum and Instruction, Educational Administration, and School Counseling support area school districts by teaching above today's state educational standards. Tarleton's own alternative-certification program, Tarleton Model for Accelerated Teacher Education (TMATE) has a long-standing history in Fort Worth and provides those with a bachelor's degree the teaching credentials and Tarleton educational experience to make a successful transition into the teaching profession.

As one of the first programs to expand to Fort Worth, Tarleton's College of Business Administration (COBA) is booming. COBA continues to expand to the Metroplex and now offers bachelor's completion degrees in accounting, computer information systems, human resources, management, and marketing. The Master of Business Administration (MBA) and Master of Science in Management and Leadership are two 36-hour graduate programs in demand due to their strong content, affordability, and flexible class options.

The degrees from the College of Liberal and Fine Arts offered at the Southwest Metroplex Center work toward building strong, community servants. The Bachelor of Social Work prepares graduates for licensure by the state for immediate entry into this demanding career field. Tarleton's Criminal Justice Program lends its support to local law enforcement through a partnership with the Fort Worth Police Department.

Criminal justice courses are offered at the department's Police Academy for both police officers and community members who wish to broaden their education.

"I'm a firm believer that education is the key element in building successful leaders for our future," says Jeffrey Halstead, Fort Worth police chief. "I am very excited about this program for community members and for the law enforcement profession."

Tarleton offers a Registered Nursing (RN)–to–Bachelor of Science in Nursing (BSN) program offered in partnership with Tarrant County College (TCC) and designed to serve licensed, working professionals in the Dallas–Fort Worth Metroplex. Geared toward those with associate-level RN degrees and those holding current, unencumbered license as a registered nurse in the United States, the program employs a blended learning approach, with classes held at the Trinity River East campus and online. Students can complete required prerequisites at TCC while enrolled at Tarleton, and those who enroll full time can complete their degree in as little as two semesters.

"Health care is changing, and this is an excellent, cost-effective opportunity to serve the high demand for BSN professionals in the Dallas–Fort Worth Metroplex," says Dr. Marilyn Duran, associate professor and director of health service professions.

In 2012 Tarleton extended its reach further into the Dallas–Fort Worth Metroplex and became a partner at the Midlothian Higher Education Center at Navarro College in Midlothian, Texas. There, Tarleton bridges the gap from community college associate degrees to bachelor's degrees to graduate degrees, offering area professionals affordable and convenient options in completing their educational goals.

For more information, visit www.tarleton.edu.

This page, from left: Tarleton provides an academically challenging educational experience through effective teaching, scholarship, research, and service. Tarleton course redesign cohorts actually dismantle and reconstruct courses to increase student interest, comprehension, and engagement. Tarleton State University President F. Dominic Dottavio, Ph.D. (far left) and Tarrant County College Vice Chancellor for Academic Affairs David Wells (far right) are pictured here with the Tarleton and TCC mascots.

Tarrant County College
The Community's College

At Tarrant County College, educators collaborate, innovate, and inspire, all in the name of providing service beyond expectations—to students on paths of opportunity, to labor markets calling for skilled workers, to business and industry searching for greater expertise, and to communities hungering for education.

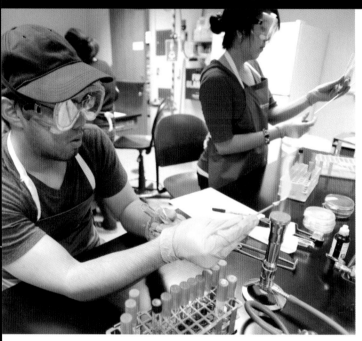

Tarrant County College (TCC) serves a world that includes a wide range of people, from single moms to corporate executives. These people all count on TCC's educators, graduates, and forward-thinking programs to empower lives with the strengths of knowledge and critical thinking. With enrollment at record levels, TCC is the sixth-largest college or university in Texas. Approximately one in every 18 Tarrant County residents takes a class at TCC each year.

Since its founding in 1965, TCC has grown from a population of 4,440 students at its first campus to more than 100,000 students today. Most are at five campuses—South, Southeast, Northeast, Northwest, and Trinity River Campus in downtown Fort Worth. Students are also immersed in studies at Trinity River East Campus for Health Care Professions, two workforce development centers, numerous learning centers countywide, and in cyberspace via TCC's online Distance Learning Program.

Class Is Always in Session

TCC's mission is to provide affordable and open access to quality teaching and learning. Its challenge is to offer those resources at the convenience of its students. Many students have full-time jobs and family responsibilities. To meet the needs of all students, flexible class schedules are offered whenever possible. Sessions range from day and evening classes to weekend classes, full-semester classes, eight-week classes, and mini-mester classes between either fall and spring semesters, spring and summer sessions, or summer and fall semesters. Customized session options tailored to meet industry needs are offered in a variety of formats. Distance Learning offers online and instructional television courses.

Offering a Wealth of Knowledge

TCC offers three types of degrees for students who plan to pursue a baccalaureate or higher degree. In addition, degrees and certificates are offered in 62 different occupational/technical programs, which include 58 Associate of Applied Science degrees and 52 certificates of completion.

TCC's Liberal Arts and Sciences degrees transfer to colleges and universities. Its Business and Industry degrees are tickets to jobs. Creative Arts degrees and certificates transfer to jobs or colleges and universities. Health Care and Community Services degrees and certificates transfer to immediate jobs or universities.

Paying It Forward

TCC ranks high among regional economic engines. The skilled workforce that TCC helped create generates more than $844.7 million in regional income as a result of students' higher earnings and impact on business activity. TCC's 3,240 faculty and staff members pump $349 million annually into Tarrant County's economy.

Through its Continuing Education Services (CES) Program, TCC responds quickly to business community needs, developing and delivering training for major businesses. This helps reduce unemployment, while allowing companies to fill shortages of skilled workers and upgrade existing employees' skills.

Continuing Education also has expanded TCC's reach throughout the county by providing nine locations, including two in Arlington, where residents can hone basic skills. Those without a high school diploma can overcome this obstacle to better-paying jobs by passing their General Educational Development (GED) test. Professional programs, courses, and seminars also are available through CES in a wide range of fields such as automotive, computers, cooking and dietetics, health care, human resources, management accounting, and small business development. Continuing Education courses include programs for senior citizens and special-needs adults.

This page: A Tarrant County College student gets fired up for the welding program on the college's South Campus.

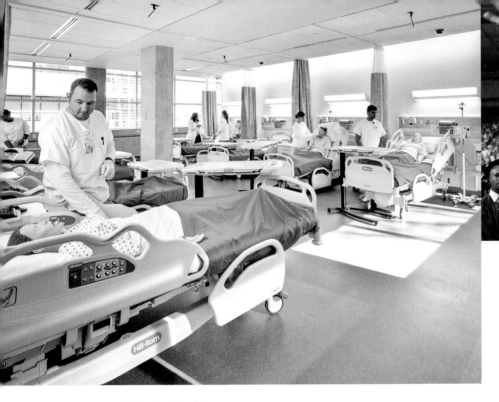

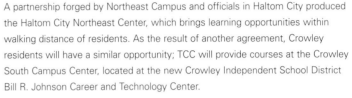

Achieving the Dream

Student success is TCC's top priority. That is why the college is part of the heralded nationwide movement Achieving the Dream: Community Colleges Count. Through Achieving the Dream, TCC uses data and engagement to focus on identifying barriers to student success, setting priorities to close student achievement gaps, developing processes for continuous improvement, and use of best practices. Achieving the Dream colleges make lasting changes in policies, programs, and services to support success for all students.

Reaching Out

TCC is committed to serving the entire community, and it does this in many nontraditional ways. For example, TCC serves the homeless through its Visions Unlimited Program, a cooperative effort with Tarrant County homeless shelter providers. The program gives homeless individuals access to higher education, aiming to build self-sufficiency among this population.

High school students can take a fast track to earning their diplomas and Associate of Arts degrees from TCC in cooperative efforts with Northwest Campus and area local independent school districts. TCC launched its first Early College High School with 38 freshmen from Lake Worth Independent School District.

A partnership forged by Northeast Campus and officials in Haltom City produced the Haltom City Northeast Center, which brings learning opportunities within walking distance of residents. As the result of another agreement, Crowley residents will have a similar opportunity; TCC will provide courses at the Crowley South Campus Center, located at the new Crowley Independent School District Bill R. Johnson Career and Technology Center.

Measures of Excellence

TCC is accredited to award associate degrees by the Southern Association of Colleges and Schools Commission on Colleges. Programs and courses are approved by the Texas Higher Education Coordinating Board. TCC also holds memberships in the Texas Association of Community Colleges, Association of Texas Colleges and Universities, and the American Association of Community Colleges.

TCC ranked number 12 in the United States in the number of associate degrees awarded in 2010, according to the national publication *Community College Weekly*. In 2011 the college ranked seventh in the number of Asian-American students, ninth in Hispanic students, and ninth in total minority students earning associate degrees in Liberal Arts and Sciences, General Studies, and Humanities, according to a report from *Diverse Issues in Higher Education*.

Some $10 million in workforce development grants were awarded to TCC from 2008 through 2012 to train nearly 10,000 workers for the local economy.

TCC's 20 state licensure programs hold an average pass rate of 95 percent, including nursing, police training, and culinary arts.

For additional information and a list of Tarrant County College program offerings, visit www.tccd.edu.

This page, from left: Nursing students train in a state-of-the-art simulated hospital using electronic "live" mannequins at the Trinity River East Campus for Health Professions. TCC graduates can transfer to a university, join the workforce, advance in their current job, or simply improve their skills thanks to the many classes available. Students at TCC's Fire Service Training Center on its Northwest Campus train in real-life situations.

TCU

TCU isn't just a university in Fort Worth—it's *the* university of Fort Worth. TCU'S mission is to educate individuals to think and act as ethical leaders and responsible citizens in the global community.

This page, from left: The heart of TCU's campus is the Campus Commons, which is bounded by four residence halls, the Brown-Lupton University Union, and Scharbauer Hall, which is home to AddRan Liberal Arts College, and the John V. Roach Honors College.

An enduring partnership was launched in 1910 when Fort Worth city fathers enticed TCU (Texas Christian University) to move from Waco to the prairie southwest of town. This century of friendship has been a boon to local business and government as scores of graduates settled in the area.

Educational Heartbeat

Today TCU's 8,300 undergraduates enjoy a rigorous, person-centered education in 130 areas of study with a student-to-faculty ratio of about 13:1. The 1,300 graduate students study in 49 master's programs and 20 areas of doctoral study. In 2011 TCU became the second-most selective college in Texas.

While the campus retains a traditional, residential atmosphere, a global perspective permeates the educational heartbeat, prompting nearly a third of the students to study abroad. Stateside partner programs such as the Schieffer Semester in Washington, D.C., provide students with hands-on intern experiences with the nation's top leaders and creators.

Over the last decade, TCU raised, then invested, more than $500 million in its future. Along with renovating and building more than two dozen facilities, the university also enhanced academic programming, increased financial aid, and hired top-flight faculty—dramatically improving its values-centered university experience. New academic facilities and an upgraded library are in the works, which will help campuswide, interdisciplinary initiatives flourish and provide new space for programs like the TCU Energy Institute and health sciences.

In 2012 the Horned Frogs joined the Big 12 athletic conference, allowing the student-athletes to again test their mettle against traditional Texas rivals and others. The Frogs won the 2011 Rose Bowl, played in their first baseball College World Series in 2010, and have earned recent national titles in equestrian and rifle. Many Frogs go on to play for professional teams and compete in the Olympics.

New facilities for soccer, track, baseball, and football now grace the 275-acre campus. Amon G. Carter Stadium was razed in 2010, and its 21st-century successor opened in fall 2012. The stadium, named for one of Fort Worth's most celebrated leaders, is an apt symbol of the symbiotic relationship between the city and its foremost university—a place where friends come to meet and champions come to play.

For more information, visit www.tcu.edu.

This page, left: Tens of thousands gather before each football game at Frog Alley, a street-fair-style venue, and the kids—known as Bleacher Creatures—dash across the field behind the team to kick off the festivities. This page, right: Graduation is always a celebration, as well as beneficial to Fort Worth: About 70,000 TCU alumni are employed locally.

UNT Health Science Center

One of the nation's distinguished academic health science centers, the UNT Health Science Center in Fort Worth is "Where the Best Begins for Health." Housed on an expansive campus in Fort Worth's Cultural District, the center is dedicated to improving the health and quality of life for the people of Texas and beyond as a leader in primary care through excellence in education, research, clinical care, and community engagement.

As one of the nation's distinguished academic health science centers, the UNT Health Science Center focuses not only on patient care and service, but also on education and research. Its graduate campus is home to 1,949 students, 400 faculty, 1,353 non-faculty staff, an alumni body 5,499 strong, and five distinct yet interwoven schools…and it is still growing. It offers small classes, an innovative curriculum, and a collaborative, inter-professional environment.

Students and faculty across the center's schools tackle bench, translational, clinical, and community-based participatory research into such issues as healthy aging, Alzheimer's disease, cardiovascular disease, cancer, vision problems, diabetes, musculoskeletal issues, health disparities, and more. Its research efforts are funded at a current total of $41 million by such groups as the National Institutes of Health (NIH), National Institute of Justice (NIJ), Department of Defense (DOD), and others.

The center's top multidisciplinary strengths are in aging and Alzheimer's disease, applied genetics, and primary care and prevention, with nationally and internationally recognized education, research, and care delivery programs. These programs reside within the center's nine-institute Health Institutes of Texas, an entity designed to translate information and research into new models of patient care and provider training. As a whole, the health science center has a local annual economic impact of more than $600 million.

The Center Then and Now

UNT Health Science Center began when the Texas College of Osteopathic Medicine accepted its first students in 1970. With the establishment of the Graduate School of Biomedical Sciences in 1993, the name was changed to the University of North Texas Health Science Center at Fort Worth.

Collectively the center offers 10 graduate degree programs and a variety of dual-degree programs. Under-represented minority students are 19 percent of total enrollment.

This page, from left: The 33-acre UNT Health Science Center campus is located in Fort Worth's well-known Cultural District. Facilities total 1.4 million square feet. The majority of UNT Health Science Center's medical students go on to practice in primary care, often in rural communities.

For more than 40 years, the UNT Health Science Center in Fort Worth has been trusted with the futures of thousands of students in medicine, biomedical sciences, public health, and health professions, and with the good health of hundreds of thousands of patients. They are, in essence, trusted with life.

To earn that trust, UNT Health Science Center must truly be the best at what it does—providing the best beginning for students on the path to becoming a doctor, researcher, public health professional, physician assistant, physical therapist, or pharmacist. It must also engage in the best research to advance progress toward prevention, treatment, and cures for individuals and communities. And it must provide the best primary and specialty care to the people of Fort Worth.

The Texas College of Osteopathic Medicine (TCOM) is among the top 50 primary care medical schools in the nation as designated by *U.S. News & World Report*— a place it has held since 2003. The Department of Family Medicine ranks 16th nationally, Geriatrics ranks 15th, and Rural Medicine ranks 12th. TCOM students have scored among the highest in the nation on all levels of the osteopathic profession's licensing exams.

Hispanic Business magazine has called TCOM one of the "Top 20 Medical Schools for Hispanics," and the *Annals of Internal Medicine* named TCOM best in Texas for social mission.

The Graduate School of Biomedical Sciences is a regional leader in training students for biomedical master's and doctorate degrees, and leads all Texas health science centers in percentage of enrolled minority students.

The School of Public Health leads the nation in student diversity and soon will offer online degree programs in addition to its campus programs.

The School of Health Professions houses the new Physical Therapy program as well as the Physician Assistant Studies program, which has been ranked among the top 50 nationally since 2003.

The UNT System College of Pharmacy is scheduled to admit its first students in fall 2013. It will be the only school of pharmacy on a health science center campus in Texas, allowing unique opportunities for students to learn alongside other future professionals who will become their partners on patient care teams.

UNT Health, the center's 250-provider faculty practice enterprise, is one of the largest multi-specialty physician groups in Tarrant County. UNT Health physicians see more than a half-million patients annually in more than 49 practice sites across the county, and deliver 7,500 babies each year.

UNT Health Science Center exists to improve the health and the quality of life for the people of Fort Worth and beyond. Through its promise to create solutions for a healthier community, it will continue to educate, conduct research, and care for North Texans long into the future. For additional information, visit www.hsc.unt.edu.

This page, clockwise from top left: Students train in a collaborative, inter-professional environment that focuses on student success. The Institute for Applied Genetics is internationally recognized for its work in human identification. The nationally ranked Texas College of Osteopathic Medicine is housed in the new Medical Education and Training building, which received a LEED Gold designation. UNT Health Science Center contributes more than $600 million annually to the local economy.

Southwestern Baptist Theological Seminary

Founded by B.H. Carroll in 1908, Southwestern Baptist Theological Seminary moved to Fort Worth in 1910 and settled on one of Tarrant County's highest points, which was quickly dubbed "Seminary Hill."

Located a few miles from the city's historic stockyards and infamous "Hell's Half Acre" downtown, the seminary changed the religious landscape of the city. Since that time, Southwestern has been served by eight presidents, beginning with Carroll and continuing to Paige Patterson, who was elected in 2003.

Southwestern's School of Theology offers graduate and doctoral degrees in pastoral, preaching, and teaching disciplines. Graduates serve as pastors, professors, missionaries, and denominational leaders. The school is home to the Center for Theological Research, the Center for Expository Preaching, the Center for Biblical Stewardship, and the Richard Land Center for Cultural Engagement.

The Roy Fish School of Evangelism and Missions offers graduate and doctoral degrees to students for service as career missionaries, evangelists, church planters, and professors. The seminary's World Mission Center sends students around the globe to proclaim the good news of Jesus Christ.

The School of Church Music leads the nation in church music education, training nearly 25 percent of the students who study church music. In addition to multiple master's degrees, Southwestern is the only school to offer a Ph.D. in church music. The school is home to the Southwestern Master Chorale and Southwestern Singers, with students performing nationally and internationally at such venues as New York's Lincoln Center.

The Jack Terry School of Church and Family Ministries offers graduate and doctoral degrees in areas such as biblical counseling, youth ministry, children's ministry, women's programs, and Christian education. Graduates serve in all levels of church ministry.

The College at Southwestern offers bachelor's degrees in biblical studies, humanities, and music. Students are introduced to major worldviews and equipped to explain and defend the truth of the Gospel.

Southwestern also offers theological education online and at its campuses in Houston, San Antonio, El Paso, Plano, and Jacksonville, Texas; as well as in Shawnee, Oklahoma; Little Rock, Arkansas; and Bonn, Germany.

The Association of Theological Schools, the Southern Association of Colleges and Schools, and the National Association of Schools of Music all accredit the seminary and its distance-learning programs. Southwestern alumni serve as pastors, teachers, music and youth ministers, counselors, chaplains, and missionaries around the world with a common heartbeat: "Preach the Word, Reach the World." www.swbts.edu

Texas Wesleyan School of Law

The only law school in Fort Worth and Tarrant County, Texas Wesleyan School of Law provides excellence in legal education to traditional full-time day students, as well as nontraditional part-time evening students.

The faculty provide students with theoretical and practical learning experiences while remaining accessible and focused on each student's success.

At Texas Wesleyan School of Law—experience is the key to success.

Graduates of the law school not only get practical, hands-on experience, but are taught by faculty members who have real-world legal experience. Texas Wesleyan Law grads are ready to hit the ground running.

Established in 1989 and located in downtown Fort Worth since 1997, Texas Wesleyan School of Law is committed to providing its students with the strong theoretical foundation and practical skills necessary to traverse the dynamic legal landscape of the 21st century. The school is located a block away from the Tarrant County Bar Association and a short distance from the legal and judicial communities of Fort Worth and Tarrant County.

The law school pursues its mission of excellence through outstanding teaching and scholarship, the development of innovative academic programs, a commitment to public service, and promotion of the highest ethical standards in the practice of law.

Extraordinary efforts are taken to not only teach legal theory, but to also prepare students for the bar exam and employment in the legal arena. Many practicum courses are designed to simulate what an attorney will face on a daily basis once admitted to the bar. The legal writing program is rigorous.

The law school prides itself on its ability to help students apply lessons learned in the classroom to real-world legal problems through its externship program, Law Clinic, and the Equal Justice Program, a mandatory 30-hour community-related pro bono requirement that must be completed by every student before graduation. To date, Texas Wesleyan students have performed more than 102,000 hours of service. With a conservative value of $25 per hour, this totals over $2.5 million of pro bono services provided to communities throughout Texas.

Texas Wesleyan is one of only 39 ABA-accredited law schools to have a pro bono graduation requirement and is also a member of the Association of American Law Schools. For more information, visit www.law.txwes.edu.

This page, above, from left: Texas Wesleyan School of Law is located in downtown Fort Worth, adjacent to the city's legal and judicial communities. The Dee J. Kelly Law Library serves as an "office" for law students, providing an extensive collection of legal resources.

PROFILES OF COMPANIES AND ORGANIZATIONS
Insurance

National Farm Life Insurance Company

With personal service a top priority, this capital stock insurance company—with almost $2.3 billion of life insurance in force throughout the state—exclusively writes life insurance policies. Established in 1946 to benefit farmers and agriculture workers, the company now serves all Texas residents.

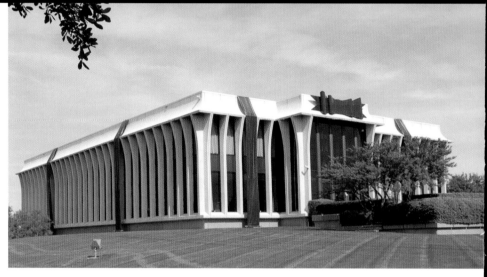

National Farm Life Insurance Company began modestly in 1946 and became the largest Texas-based life insurance company that markets only to Texas residents. National Farm Life provides high-quality insurance coverage at the lowest possible cost.

William C. "Brigham" Young founded the company in Fort Worth to provide life insurance for professional agriculture workers. He started in an office borrowed from a friend, and soon moved his growing company into the original Stockyards National Bank, located in Fort Worth's historic stockyards. National Farm Life expanded in the 1950s to extend its services to all Texas residents. Even though the company has now encompassed the urban market, a substantial percentage of National Farm Life's policyholders still live in rural areas.

In 1968 National Farm Life moved its Home Office to the east side of Fort Worth, on a 20-acre tract near the interstate highway that links the city to Dallas. Even residents and visitors unfamiliar with National Farm Life probably know the company's building well—it sits atop a hill on Bridge Street, just north of Interstate 30. For many Fort Worth residents, the building symbolizes the Christmas spirit and the holidays. When National Farm Life held its open house and ribbon-cutting ceremony in 1968, it decorated its building with a red bow and streaming red ribbons, which gave the building the appearance of a giant present. The ribbons and bow became a tradition, and the building became a landmark for commuters and travelers along the Dallas–Fort Worth interstate. Every holiday season, National Farm Life meticulously drapes six red ribbons, each 54 feet long and four feet wide, over the building and hoists a giant 350-pound, 22-foot-long red bow above the front entrance.

Success Founded on Stability

National Farm Life has more than $300 million in assets and has been unique among life insurance companies in structuring shareholders' dividends.

Stockholder dividends are limited to 10 percent of the original stock purchase price, or a maximum of $14,000 a year. All additional earnings are dedicated either to pay policyholder dividends or remain for the financial security of policyholders. The company declared almost $3.2 million in policyholder dividends in 2011. Since 1946, National Farm Life has provided its policyholders with over $79 million in dividends and has paid more than $86 million in death benefits to beneficiaries.

National Farm Life is managed by Chairman, President, and CEO J. D. "Chip" Davis and Marketing Executive Vice President Cary L. Wright. Senior Vice Presidents are Mark Bigsby and Richard Jernigan. Other Vice Presidents are Linda Huens, Mark Williams, and Lenay Pacheco. Collectively, these officers have amassed 210 years

with National Farm Life. In the company's history, there have been only four presidents: Donald L. Jones, Sr. (1946–1974), Donald L. Jones, Jr. (1974–1999), Ronald G. Downing (1999–2004), and Chip Davis (2005–present).

National Farm Life has almost $2.3 billion of life insurance in force throughout Texas. The company has five state coordinators: Recruiting Director Dale Raburn, from Lubbock; Area Coordinator Scott Anderson, from Hubbard; Area Coordinator Glen Baecker, CLU, from Austin; Area Coordinator Coy Worden, from Kaufman; and American Farm Life's Regional Coordinator Jimmy James, from Oklahoma.

Success in the Community

In addition to its business successes, National Farm Life contributes significantly toward the stability of its community through a variety of activities and organizations. National Farm Life is involved in the Boy Scouts of America, the East Fort Worth Business Association, and the Fort Worth Adopt-A-School Program. The company also belongs to the Texas Association of Life and Health Insurers and the American Council of Life Insurers. In 2000 National Farm Life formed the American Farm Life Insurance Company, which is licensed in Texas, Oklahoma, and New Mexico.

Since 1946, National Farm Life has served the life insurance needs of Texas residents with integrity, efficiency, and conservancy. Its future success will stem from adhering to those same principles. National Farm Life Insurance Company has attained a position of prominence, not only in Fort Worth, but also in the insurance industry. For more information, visit www.nflic.com.

2011 National Farm Life Insurance Company President's Cabinet

Randy Robertson, Lubbock	Gary Kneip, Edna	Mike Hill, Midland	Sam LeNoir, Groesbeck
Allen Jolly, Lubbock	Don David Hutto, Waco	Paul Jones, Abilene	Steve Kosadnar, LUTCF, Athens
John Rosser, Lubbock	Jimmie Berry, Manor	Laura Magee, El Paso	Patricia Torres, Odessa
Donna Anderson, Hubbard	Kelly Springer, LUTCF, Amarillo	Teressia Marley, Girard	Scott Yarbrough, San Marcos
Donnie Prater, Tulia	Shirley Clark, Amarillo	Benny Thomas, Lubbock	Joyce VanNess, Levelland
Jim Embrey, LUTCF, Waco	Frank McCullough, Pampa	Larry Hankins, Garland	Edward Barela, Midland
Jim Thomas, Lubbock	Russ Wright, Girard	John Esquivel, McAllen	Virginia Mendez, Amarillo
Sergio Ceja, Lubbock	Joe Rosser, LUTCF, The Woodlands	Shere Forbes, LUTCF, Brownfield	Carol Metteauer, Palestine
Michael Light, Brownwood	Bobby Sisemore, LUTCF, Kress	Jerry Knight, Sulphur Springs	

PROFILES OF COMPANIES AND ORGANIZATIONS
Pharmaceuticals

Galderma

Founded in 1981 as a joint venture between Nestlé and L'Oréal, Galderma is a global pharmaceutical company exclusively focused on dermatology. Galderma has over 4,000 employees around the world and 31 wholly owned affiliates, including Galderma Laboratories, L.P., the U.S. headquarters in Fort Worth.

This page: Galderma's U.S. headquarters has been in North Fort Worth, near Fort Worth Alliance Airport and the Texas Motor Speedway, since November 2000. The company's U.S. operations were originally established in Dallas in 1961 as Owen Laboratories. Owen was then acquired by Fort Worth–based Alcon Laboratories in 1972 and became part of Swiss-based food giant Nestlé in 1977. Galderma was created in 1981 through a joint venture of worldwide leaders Nestlé and L'Oréal.

Galderma is committed to delivering innovative medical solutions to meet the dermatological needs of people throughout their lifetime, while also serving health care professionals around the world. The company provides a portfolio of prescription, over-the-counter, and aesthetic and corrective solutions to support lifelong challenges of skin conditions.

In the United States, Galderma is recognized as the number one dermatology company by various independent surveys for the quality of its products, marketing, and medical programs, as well as its research and development and sales team performance.*

Galderma has grown its staff in the United States by more than 6.5 percent since 2007, with its 2012 headcount expected to approach 600. Approximately 250 of these employees are based in Fort Worth. In the Dallas/Fort Worth area, Galderma hires talented individuals with credentials from top-notch educational institutions that include local universities such as Texas Christian University, the University of North Texas, the University of Texas at Arlington, and Southern Methodist University, as well as other respected, Texas-based universities such as the University of Texas at Austin, Texas A&M University, Baylor University, and Texas Tech University.

Meeting People's Dermatological Needs for a Lifetime

"At Galderma, patients and health care professionals are at the heart of everything we do. Galderma provides medical solutions for everyone throughout all stages of life," explains François Fournier, president of Galderma's U.S. and Canadian operations.

Strategic brands in the United States include Epiduo®, Oracea®, Clobex®, Differin®, MetroGel®, Vectical®, Cetaphil®, and Pliaglis® for aesthetic and corrective activities. The Cetaphil line is among Galderma's top products. One Cetaphil Gentle Skin Cleanser product is sold every 10 seconds. One Cetaphil product unit is sold every second.

Source: SDI Company Image Survey—results in Dermatology, 2011.

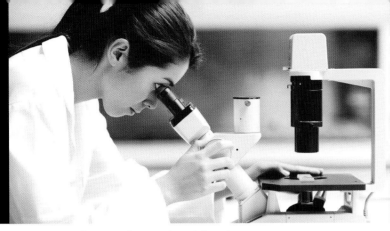

Dermatology-focused Research and Development

The Galderma organization focuses its global unique scientific and medical capabilities on dermatology. With approximately 19 percent of revenues invested each year to discover and develop new products and access innovative technologies, the company is one of the world's leading investors in dermatology research and development.

Four state-of-the-art research and development centers are dedicated to providing a wide range of innovative medical solutions, which meet the highest standards of safety and efficacy. Galderma's research center at Sophia Antipolis in France is one of the largest dermatology research sites in the world. This leading-edge laboratory is supported by clinical development centers in Princeton, New Jersey, and Tokyo, Japan. The Center of Excellence in Uppsala, Sweden, is dedicated to aesthetic and corrective dermatology research.

Unyielding Support for Dermatology

For more than 30 years, Galderma has collaborated with dermatologists, health care professionals, dermatological and medical institutions, and nonprofit research foundations in the United States and worldwide.

Galderma is an active supporter of multiple patient and physician advocacy groups, such as the American Academy of Dermatology, the American Academy of Pediatrics, the Dermatology Foundation, and Dermatology residents. In 2009 the Baylor Dermatology Residency program in North Texas was initiated in part by a grant from Galderma. The program's objective is to train new dermatologists and help stem the shortage of specialists in the Lone Star State. Over the last

32 years, an estimated 80 percent of all U.S. dermatologists have taken the Galderma Pre-Board Seminar, a board-certification preparatory course.

Galderma has also committed annual funding to raise public awareness of skin disease using campaigns via television, the Internet, and informational school programs. Through its Cetaphil brand, the company supports the Children's Skin Disease Foundation, including Camp Wonder for children with severe skin diseases.

Supporting North Texas Communities

Galderma is also committed to supporting charitable organizations that contribute to the good of the local community through grants and product donations. The company contributes to summer camps for children with skin conditions, like "Camp Braveskin," south of Dallas. Galderma also supports local charities like "First Command Package Brigade™" in Fort Worth, which collects donations for American military serving overseas. Cetaphil products are included in many care packages sent to active military.

Galderma also fosters children's education via grants to local organizations such as the Amon Carter Museum of American Art in Fort Worth. In 2012 Galderma sponsored "Story Time," a free community reading program that benefited more than 3,000 children.

For additional information about Galderma, visit the company's Web site at www.galdermausa.com.

Above left: Approximately 19 percent of Galderma revenues are invested each year to develop new products and access innovative technologies. The company is one of the world's leading investors in dermatology research and development. Above right: Galderma's innovative medical solutions meet dermatological needs of people around the world, helping improve their quality of life.

Left: Galderma's U.S. product lines include Cetaphil®, Clobex®, Epiduo®, Differin®, MetroGel®, Oracea®, Vectical®, and Pliaglis®. Consumers are encouraged to report negative side effects of prescription drugs to the FDA. Visit www.fda.gov/medwatch or 1-800-FDA-1088.

PROFILES OF COMPANIES AND ORGANIZATIONS
Professional Services

Freese and Nichols

Freese and Nichols began in Fort Worth in 1894, and the company's engineers and architects have shaped Fort Worth's infrastructure ever since. Founder Major John B. Hawley designed the main pump station for the Holly Water Treatment Plant that served as the City's first water system.

This page, from above left: Freese and Nichols designed the Phyllis J. Tilley Pedestrian Bridge (in collaboration with Rosales + Partners and Schlaich Bergermann und Partner), connecting downtown Fort Worth to the City's cultural district. Freese and Nichols' delegation at the Malcolm Baldrige National Quality Award ceremony (left to right): Robert Pence, Jim Nichols, Cindy Milrany, U.S. Congresswoman Kay Granger, Fort Worth Mayor Betsy Price, and Lee Freese.

Freese and Nichols' Fort Worth–area projects encompass the full gamut of the firm's professional services in engineering, architecture, environmental science, planning, construction services, and program management:

- Program management of DFW International Airport's Terminal Renewal and Improvement Program
- Design of Phyllis J. Tilley Pedestrian Bridge, Clearfork Main Street Bridge, and Trinity River Vision Bridges in Fort Worth
- Engineering and program management of natural gas transmission lines and facilities throughout the Barnett Shale
- Primary consultant for Region C Water Plan, the long-term plan for North Texas
- Design, construction management, and continuous improvements at the Holly Water Treatment Plant since 1894
- Route selection and design of three earthen balancing reservoirs and a 12-mile pipeline segment for the $1.6-billion Integrated Pipeline Project, delivering water from East Texas to North Texas
- Master planning for downtown Fort Worth
- Design of Fort Worth Water Gardens Improvements

- Design and permitting for dredging of Lake Worth
- Update of City's wastewater master plan
- Design and construction management of The Women's Center of Tarrant County
- Design of the Energy Technology Center, Tarrant County College South Campus

Freese and Nichols is a charter member of the Institute of Sustainable Infrastructure, and employees hold leadership positions on national boards for sustainability organizations. Employees also take action in the community. Since 2007, employees have logged 33,255 volunteer hours to community organizations throughout Texas.

Notable awards over the past five years include:

- Tarrant County and American Business Ethics Award, Foundation for Financial Service Professionals, 2007
- Malcolm Baldrige National Quality Award, National Institute of Standards and Technology, 2010
- Vision 20/20 Award for Best Places to Work Overall for Young Professionals, Fort Worth Chamber of Commerce, 2010
- Best Civil Engineering Firm to Work For (large firm) and Ranked #5 Among Top Engineering Firms in the Country, CE News, 2011
- CEO of the Year (private company), awarded to President Robert Pence, P.E., BCEE, Fort Worth Business Press, 2011
- CFO of the Year (medium-size company), awarded to Cindy Milrany, CPA, Fort Worth Business Press, 2012

Headquartered in Fort Worth, Freese and Nichols has 15 offices with 500-plus employees throughout the state.

For more information about the company's projects and services, visit www.freese.com.

Jackson Walker L.L.P.

Jackson Walker L.L.P. has a long and rich history in Texas that includes deep roots in Fort Worth. The law firm, which recently celebrated its 125th anniversary, is the largest Texas-only firm, with more than 340 attorneys in seven offices. Its clients include some of the biggest companies in the world, as well as smaller companies, family-owned businesses, individuals, and nonprofits.

Throughout its history, Jackson Walker has supported the growth and development of Texas by representing notable clients in industries such as railroads, real estate, and oil and gas. Jackson Walker's deep connection with Fort Worth, in particular, is revealed in the name of the city's prominent Lancaster Avenue. In 1931 the road then called "Texas Street" was renamed for John L. Lancaster, president of the Texas & Pacific Railway. Lancaster's son was a name partner at Jackson Walker, and his grandson, John L. Lancaster III, is a respected trial attorney who still practices at the firm. Jackson Walker continues to play a key role in Fort Worth business today through its representation of clients that include Crescent Real Estate Equities, Chesapeake Energy, and Texas Health Resources.

Jackson Walker's commitment to the community is also seen in its longstanding involvement with the Fort Worth Chamber of Commerce. Partner Susan Halsey, who leads Jackson Walker's Fort Worth office, serves as Chamber vice chairman and will serve as chairman in 2013-14. Halsey is consistently recognized as one of Tarrant County's top real estate attorneys, as a result of both her legal expertise and her tireless commitment to the community. In addition to her work with the Chamber, Halsey is a past chairman of the Greater Fort Worth Real Estate Council and recently received that organization's Founder's Award in recognition of her leadership within the Fort Worth real estate industry.

Partner Albon Head is also deeply involved in civic and charitable activities, having served as a director and past chairman of the Fort Worth Chamber, as well as past president of the Fort Worth Opera, and past chairman of YMCA Camp Amon G. Carter. In his legal career, Head has more than 40 years of experience representing clients in a wide variety of litigation matters. He has done high-profile work for the Texas Rangers, assisting in the team's purchase and operation of the franchise during the mid-1970s and handling litigation and related matters during the George W. Bush ownership era.

As Jackson Walker has grown with its clients over the past 125 years, it has remained true to its Texas roots and maintained the uniquely collegial culture for which it is known. The firm is proud to be a part of Fort Worth's heritage and looks forward to serving the community for many years to come.

For additional information, visit www.jw.com.

This page, from left: Jackson Walker partner Susan Halsey heads the firm's Fort Worth office and is the 2013-14 chairman of the Fort Worth Chamber of Commerce; Partner Albon Head is past chairman of the Fort Worth Chamber.

Open Channels Group, LLC

A Fort Worth–based, full-service public relations agency, Open Channels Group specializes in multicultural, public participation, and digital.

Innovative. Energetic. Collaborative. Savvy.

Those are just a few words used to describe Open Channels Group (OCG), an emerging, forward-thinking public relations agency. The OCG team values collaborative partnerships with its clients to help them connect with the diverse communities and customers they serve. A woman- and minority-owned company based in downtown Fort Worth, OCG serves a growing list of public, private, and not-for-profit businesses and organizations. OCG's mission is to give voice to the clients it serves.

History and Experience

OCG was founded in 2005 by Fort Worth native Tonya Veasey. OCG has served more than 30 clients in a range of industries, including energy, health care, telecommunications, transportation, sports, family entertainment, and recycling.

OCG's award-winning work includes multicultural communications, news media and blogger relations, message development, technical writing, branding, and communications planning. As OCG continues to grow and serve more clients, the company has evolved into a full-service PR agency, offering an array of digital and social media services to complement its traditional public relations practice.

OCG is well-respected for its Public Participation (P2) practice, as well. The P2 team excels at working with public entities to maximize public input, facilitate stakeholder participation in public projects, and engage the public in the decision-making process. OCG has managed the P2 process for a number of major public projects in North Texas.

Tonya Veasey, President and founder of Open Channels Group, directs a communications strategy session for a client.

Giving Back

With deep roots in Fort Worth and a strong commitment to the community, OCG allocates staff time and resources to assist a not-for-profit client on a pro bono basis each year. Past pro bono clients include Fort Worth's Day Resource Center, which works with the homeless population, and Recovery

Resource Council, Tarrant County's leading resource for drug and alcohol abuse treatment and prevention.

Says founder and President Veasey: "At OCG, our goal is pretty simple—we tell our clients to set high expectations of us, and then we go to work to exceed those expectations. No matter how much we continue to grow, we will always work to provide the individualized attention that each client needs to advance its business objectives."

For more information, visit www.openchannelsgroup.com, Facebook.com/OpenChannelsGroup, and Twitter.com/OpenChannelsPR.

PROFILES OF COMPANIES AND ORGANIZATIONS
Real Estate

Mercantile Center

Strategically located within the Dallas/Fort Worth Metroplex, Mercantile Center is one of Fort Worth's most prestigious business parks, designed for companies looking for a centralized location and state-of-the-art facilities. With three local international airports and interstate highway access, Mercantile Center is just minutes from regional, national, and global connections.

Interstate 820 North and just minutes from Dallas/Fort Worth International Airport. Home to the Federal Aviation Administration's regional headquarters, the center has attracted a number of other high-profile tenants, including CitiGroup, Dillard's, Medtronic, OmniAmerican Bank, Sara Lee, Sprint, Trane, and TTI.

Mercantile Center is situated in an Enterprise Zone, a Foreign Trade Zone, and a Triple Freeport Enterprise area. These incentives offer the potential for significant savings for companies and organizations that locate here.

Mercantile Center has enjoyed steady growth over the past 25 years, paralleling the growth of the Fort Worth area. Distribution centers provide 20,000 to 137,000 square feet of modern warehouse space.

Tech Center VII offers unique and highly functional flex/tech space, while Mercantile Plaza and Mercantile Center One offer more traditional office environments.

With occupancy at 95 percent, Mercantile Partners, the developer for Mercantile Center, has launched an expansion project designed to help further Fort Worth's role as one of the nation's leading distribution centers. Called Mercantile Distribution Center 5 and 6, these state-of-the-art office/warehouse buildings are each 94,000 square feet with 28 dock doors.

Committed to the City of Fort Worth and the surrounding areas, Mercantile Center plans to continue to develop the center into a high-quality business park that reflects the growing needs of existing and potential clients. Says Brian Randolph, Mercantile Vice President, "We believe the future of Fort Worth is a bright one, and Mercantile Center is poised to play a prominent role in our community's future growth."

For more information, visit www.mercantilecenter.com.

Above: Spanning more than 1,500 acres, Mercantile Center offers prime industrial and office locations within minutes of downtown Fort Worth.

Forty years ago, the farmland of north-central Tarrant County seemed an unlikely site for a business park. But a visionary group of developers recognized its potential to serve the needs of a region that was about to experience an explosion in population growth and business expansion.

The result of their vision was Mercantile Center, a 1,500-acre master-planned business park in north Fort Worth that provides space for industrial, office, and service organizations. Strategically positioned to attract businesses to the Fort Worth area, the center is located on Interstate 35 West, a half mile south of

Williams Trew Sotheby's International Realty

A residential real estate firm based in Fort Worth, Williams Trew Sotheby's International Realty is dedicated to the needs of the individuals and families it represents.

Founded in Fort Worth in 2000, Williams Trew offers the unique perspective that comes from being based in its hometown. Committed to treating each client with respect and focused attention in every interaction, the agency strives to exceed expectations through use of innovative technology resources, comprehensive marketing strategies, and a full-service approach.

Williams Trew agents are selectively chosen for their experience, professionalism, and understanding of the real estate industry and the local communities in which they serve. Williams Trew has 80 agents in its two Fort Worth offices. Providing the highest level of experience, service, and dedication, the agents have an average experience of more than 12 years, with average sales per agent exceeding $5.5 million a year. From downtown lofts and condos to luxury homes and vacation properties to ranch and hunting properties, Williams Trew can match its clients with the listing best suited to their lifestyles and budgets.

In April 2012 Williams Trew became an Affiliate of Sotheby's International Realty, a brand known worldwide for its ability to market luxury residential properties. As a member of the Sotheby's network of high-profile agencies around the world, Williams Trew can offer its clients' homes greater exposure on hundreds of Web sites and in a variety of high-end publications.

"We have been a leader in residential sales since our inception, and combining forces with the Sotheby's International Realty brand will allow us to reach beyond our current scope, providing us the tools and abilities needed to enhance our dedication and service to the area we love," said Williams Trew co-owner Martha Williams.

That Williams Trew was well-established in Fort Worth, a high-growth community, made it an attractive choice for Sotheby's. Michael Good, CEO of Sotheby's International Realty Affiliates, said, "Williams Trew has an established record of excellence, having served the luxury market since the firm's inception in 2000, and we are proud to have them represent us in this critical market."

With its local knowledge, presence, and strength in the Fort Worth market, Williams Trew is perfectly positioned to serve the needs of its clients for many years to come.

For more information, visit www.williamstrew.com.

Above, from left:
Lobby of Williams Trew;
Martha Williams and
Joan Trew (left to right);
Fort Worth skyline.

PROFILES OF COMPANIES AND ORGANIZATIONS
Retail

Pier 1 Imports®

Based in Fort Worth, Texas, Pier 1 Imports is the original global importer of unique decorative home furnishings and gifts. In 2012 Pier 1 Imports celebrated its Golden Anniversary.

The Journey

It has been more than 50 years since the well-loved Pier 1 Imports® company was founded and its first store opened in San Mateo, CA, in November 1962. Since then, Pier 1 Imports has grown to more than 1,000 locations in 49 states and Canada. Pier 1 Imports also offers products at select Sears de Mexico "boutique locations" in Mexico.

Today Pier 1 Imports employs approximately 19,000 associates across North America, including the more than 600 associates who work at the corporate headquarters. 2012 marked the company's 40th year listed on the New York Stock Exchange (NYSE) under the stock symbol PIR.

The Merchandise

Pier 1 Imports' authentic and distinctive merchandise reflects the diverse cultures of the many countries its buyers explore. A broad assortment of items and styles offers something for everyone—useful, decorative, and the purely whimsical. From initial product development to store display, Pier 1 Imports' merchandise is carefully chosen to provide exclusive, one-of-a-kind items that offer excellent quality at a great value. The process begins with the buyers, who travel the world searching for colorful, unique merchandise with a global, artisan feel, including hand-painted dinnerware, rich textiles, home fragrance, wall décor, and indoor and outdoor furniture.

The Stores

Pier 1 Imports offers a special shopping experience, whether in store or online, where customers can find long-time favorites as well as something new. Stores are a treat for the senses. Fragrant candles, the colors and patterns of dinnerware, textured carvings, and woven textiles all combine to create an eclectic environment. The company's Visual Merchandising Team designs unique merchandise displays in store layouts that are easy to explore and merchandise vignettes that are eye-catching. Products are accessible, inviting shoppers to touch, hold, and imagine them in their homes. Most important, Pier 1 Imports' associates bring the brand to life with their creativity, talent, and dedication to helping each customer reflect his or her personal style every day. Associates engage customers sincerely

This page: More than 1,000 Pier 1 Imports® stores are found throughout North America. Opposite page, from left: The original Pier 1 Imports store was founded in 1962. Shoppers can find beautiful and unique decorative accessories at Pier 1 Imports stores. Pier 1 Imports associates are always ready to help customers find what they need.

THE PIER 1 IMPORTS JOURNEY

1962
Pier 1 Imports starts as a single store in San Mateo, California, in 1962. First customers are post–World War II baby boomers looking for beanbag chairs, love beads, and incense. Pier 1 Imports has carried a wide selection of merchandise through the years, from chocolate-covered ants to clothing lines to life-size Spanish suits of armor.

1966
Pier 1 Imports establishes corporate headquarters in Fort Worth, Texas, and has

16 store locations with a merchandise mix of incense and other popular novelty items of the time.

1970
Pier 1 Imports goes public and becomes listed on the American Stock Exchange.

1972
The company joins the New York Stock Exchange under the stock ticker symbol PIR. By this time, Pier 1 Imports has 124 stores, including stores in Australia and Europe, and

celebrates 100 percent sales gains for four consecutive years.

1979
A Pier 1 Imports store in Royal Oak, Michigan, is the first to reach $1 million in annual sales.

1985
With 265 stores, the company hones its image as a retailer of quality, unique home furnishings, and decorative accessories; a plan is launched to double the number of stores over five years.

1988
The Pier 1 Preferred Card is introduced and within six years Preferred Card sales reach $100 million.

1993
Pier 1 Imports expands into Puerto Rico; begins a partnership with The Pier, a chain of retail import stores in the United Kingdom; and opens boutiques in Sears de Mexico stores.

and strive to make customers' experience with Pier 1 Imports a treat, giving them lots of reasons to come back soon and often.

The Headquarters

Pier 1 Imports' corporate headquarters is located in a beautiful 460,000-square-foot, 20-story building on more than 14 acres of land in the Trinity Riverfront, a landmark improvement project in Fort Worth. The building features a conference center, an information systems and training center, and amenities for associates such as a fitness center, walking trail, and on-site café.

The Community

Pier 1 Imports recognizes its global citizenship, and associates strive to go about their business in a way that makes them proud. Where and when they are able, Pier 1 Imports associates help the community in which they work and live.

Since 1985 Pier 1 Imports has contributed more than $44 million to philanthropic organizations, including the United Nations Children's Fund (UNICEF), the United Way of Tarrant County, and the Adopt-A-School program with E.M. Daggett Elementary School.

Pier 1 Imports, which has raised nearly $34 million for UNICEF, has partnered with the international children's relief organization in an annual greeting card contest in both the U.S. and Canada. Children submit their hand-drawn pictures based on an annual holiday contest theme, and the winning artwork is reproduced as official UNICEF greeting cards sold at all Pier 1 Imports locations to benefit children around the world.

The company also supports the United Way of Tarrant County in its goal to improve the lives of many in the community through its three main initiatives of education, financial stability, and health. Over the past 28 years, Pier 1 Imports and its associates have donated more than $10 million to the United Way of Tarrant County.

Pier 1 Imports has been an adopter of E.M. Daggett Elementary since 1986. The partnership has won the Fort Worth Independent School District's Exemplary Partnership Award, the district's highest honor, three times. Associates support Daggett through the annual Daggett Elementary Clothing Closet and various educational programs throughout the year.

The Culture

Pier 1 Imports credits its associates with creating a unique and special personality for the company, which has been a vital part of its success story. The culture is about associates' attitude toward business, how they think, and their expectations. It's about how associates behave and treat each other and their day-in and day-out demeanor as they go about their work. Everyone at Pier 1 Imports is committed to being successful as a business while also living their values every day—challenging each other, supporting each other, and fostering a friendly and open environment where they can all feel fulfilled.

The culture, like the merchandise, at Pier 1 Imports, continues to evolve as the company looks to the next 50 years with optimism and confidence that there is only one authentic global importer that brings the world home for its customers—the ever-original, ever-evolving Pier 1 Imports. For more information, visit www.pier1.com.

1999
A critical pricing and merchandising repositioning strategy brings Pier 1 Imports back in touch with its core customers. For the first time, sales reach $1 billion.

2000
The company launches its online store at pier1.com and a new advertising campaign. The "Get In Touch With Your Senses" campaign positions Pier 1 Imports as a fun, sensory shopping experience that customers had long identified with the eclectic specialty store. Kirstie Alley serves as first-time celebrity spokesperson for the company.

2001
Pier 1 Imports acquires Cargo Furniture and Home and changes the concept into Pier 1 Kids, a specialty retailer offering value-oriented, fashionable children's furniture and accessories.

2002
Pier 1 Imports celebrates its 40-year history of retailing.

2003
The company opens its 1,000th North American store in Summerlin, a master-planned community in Las Vegas, Nevada.

2004
Pier 1 Imports transitions from three downtown Fort Worth office locations and moves Home Office associates into new corporate headquarters along the Trinity River. The company also announces a new marketing campaign designed to remind customers of the globally inspired, one-of-a kind mix of home furnishings and accessories offered, and the exciting in-store experience discovered when shopping at Pier 1 Imports.

2005
The company records its highest annual net sales by topping $1.9 billion.

2007
Pier 1 Imports restructures, survives the recession, and comes out strong three years later.

2011
The company announces its three-year growth plan designed to drive sales, further improve profitability, and return value to its shareholders.

2012
Pier 1 Imports ends its fiscal year by reporting merchandise margins over 59 percent of sales; launches new e-Commerce site, Pier 1 To-You; celebrates its 50-year history of retailing; is invited to ring the NYSE closing bell in celebration of its 40th year of being listed on the stock exchange.

RadioShack®

Through a vast network of nearly 7,300 U.S. and international locations, RadioShack offers a broad range of electronic products, accessories, and services that today's consumers need to keep their connected lives running smoothly.

RadioShack offers innovative mobile devices, consumer electronics, and personal technology from leading national brands, as well as its exclusive private brands. Customers can choose from a full complement of postpaid services from three leading national carriers—Verizon Wireless, AT&T, and Sprint—along with leading national prepaid providers.

Combining the purchasing power of a national retailer with the personal touch of a neighborhood merchant, RadioShack stores provide an inviting, nearby small-store format along with an unbiased sales approach and expert advice that not only covers wireless and mobility, but a range of electronics accessories and technical products for hobbyists.

RadioShack's Trade & Save Program allows customers to trade in retired mobile phones and other electronic devices to receive immediate store credit for purchases. RadioShack accepts eligible devices on trade-in no matter where the customer first purchased them. Retired devices are recycled, refurbished for resale, or disposed of responsibly, minimizing the volume of electronic material in the waste stream.

The name came from the small wooden structure that housed radio equipment aboard ships. The first RadioShack opened in Boston in 1921, supplying ship radio equipment and ham radios. In 1963 Tandy Corporation of Fort Worth, which had started life in 1919 as a leather goods supplier, acquired the struggling company, transforming it into a worldwide leader in retail electronics. In 2000 Tandy Corporation changed its name to RadioShack Corporation.

This page: Based in Fort Worth, RadioShack has about 4,700 stores in the United States and Mexico.

Based in Fort Worth, RadioShack is a multibillion-dollar company operating approximately 4,700 stores in the United States and Mexico, along with nearly 1,500 wireless phone centers in the United States and more than 1,100 dealer and other outlets worldwide. The company employs approximately 34,000 people globally.

RadioShack continues to expand its global footprint, offering the small-format consumer electronics retail experience internationally in association with local experts. RadioShack plans to expand across 10 Southeast Asian countries through a master development agreement with a Malaysian retail group. Further expansion into the People's Republic of China is planned through a joint venture with a local market expert. International expansion gives RadioShack the opportunity to broaden its brand reach and leverage its strong brand identity.

For more information about the company, visit radioshackcorporation.com.

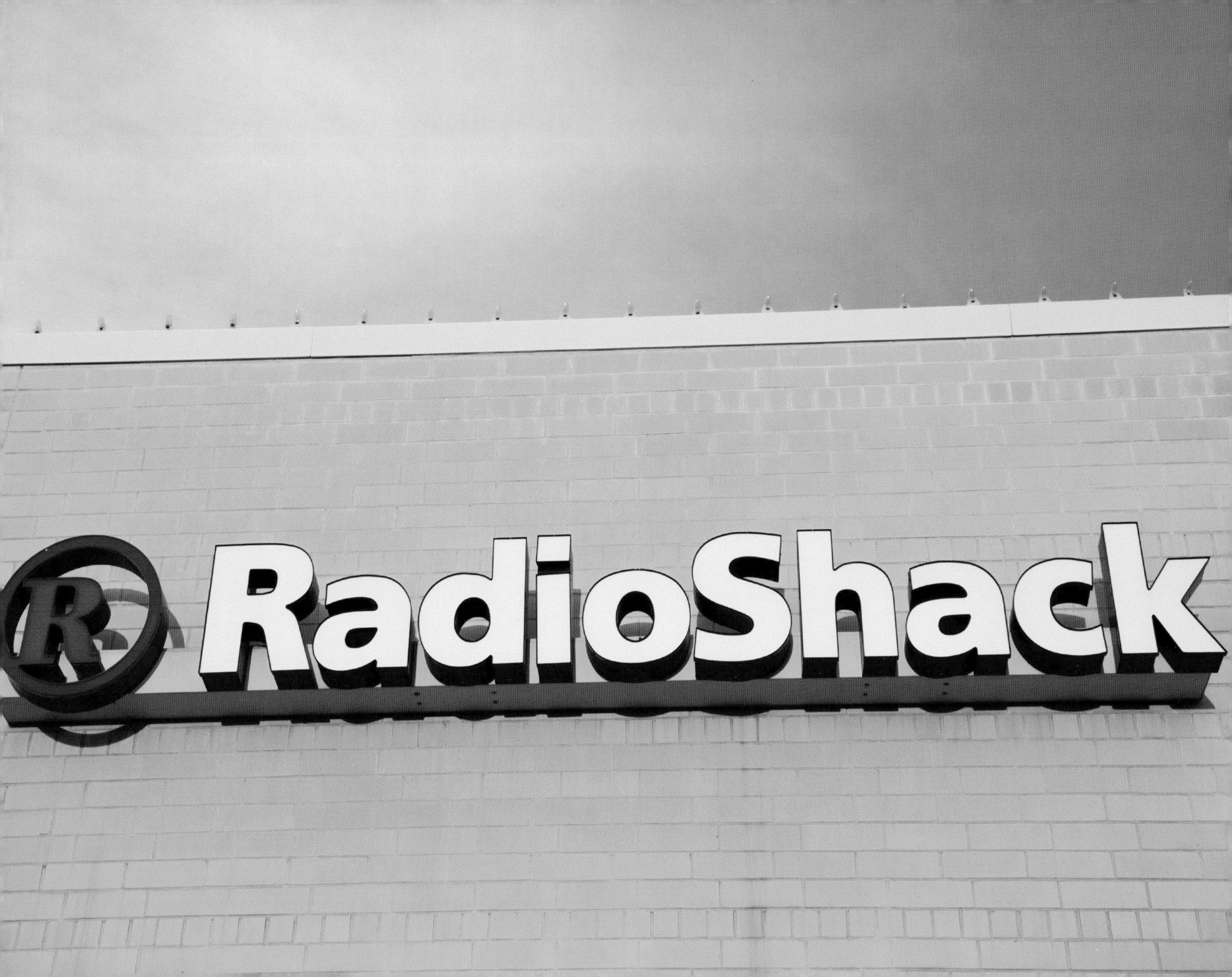
RadioShack

PROFILES OF COMPANIES AND ORGANIZATIONS
Transportation, Distribution, & Logistics

BNSF: At Home in Fort Worth

With a rich history spanning more than 160 years, BNSF Railway plays a vital role in the Texas economy, employing 6,800 people in Texas and moving four million carloads of freight across the state each year, which helps reduce highway congestion and harmful emissions. Fort Worth is home to BNSF's s corporate headquarters, where the company employs more than 4,500 Dallas–Fort Worth residents.

Providing a Vital Link

BNSF Railway is one of the largest railroads in North America, serving 28 states and two Canadian provinces. BNSF provides a vital link to the U.S. economy by connecting producers and consumers and helps move more freight more efficiently and more safely than any other mode of surface transportation.

Today BNSF has grown into a company that employs approximately 40,000 people, has an average annual capital investment of $2.6 billion, and ships more than 9.5 million carloads annually. Moving everything from the products that consumers use every day to the raw materials and supplies that manufacturers need to make those goods, BNSF connects manufacturers to consumers and farmers to families.

The demand for rail freight is growing in importance every day. The U.S. Department of Transportation projects that the demand for rail freight transportation will increase 88 percent by 2035. With this in mind, BNSF is constantly innovating at its Fort Worth headquarters to stay at the forefront of what's next.

Investing in Texas' Future

Fort Worth is also home to BNSF's network operations center for train dispatching and network operations. Nearly 15 percent of BNSF's 32,000-mile rail network is in Texas. In addition, Fort Worth hosts BNSF's first Logistics Park concept, a freight

development model pioneered by BNSF and Hillwood in which distribution centers and warehouses are developed near intermodal facilities. Logistics Parks are a 21st-century development concept that provides a competitive advantage to a shipper's supply chain, significantly reducing local truck trips between intermodal and distribution facilities.

The Logistics Park idea was first developed in Fort Worth, and since its initial creation, this model has been used to develop similar Logistics Parks near Chicago, Memphis, and Kansas City, resulting in the creation of thousands of new jobs and several billion dollars in economic development.

As an industry leader in protecting the environment and improving safety, BNSF also generates some of the best-paying jobs in the communities it serves. In Texas alone, BNSF has an annual payroll of more than $682 million.

Expanding Infrastructure

BNSF has continued to expand its Fort Worth and Texas infrastructure and facilities in response to growing market demand. In a three-year span, BNSF invested more than $818 million in Texas for capacity expansion and maintenance. Among BNSF's key projects is supporting major enhancements to Tower 55, one of the busiest and most congested railroad intersections in the country. Located near downtown Fort Worth, Tower 55 hosts more

Left: The network operations center, based in Fort Worth at BNSF's corporate headquarters, dispatches trains and helps keep the network running. Opposite page: BNSF Railway is one of the largest railroads in North America, with nearly 15 percent of its 32,000-mile rail network in Texas.

than 100 trains per day and provides connectivity for freight and passenger travel between the West Coast, Midwest, Southeast, Canada, and Mexico.

In addition to the significant financial contributions being made by the railroads, the North Texas Council of Governments, the City of Fort Worth, the Texas Department of Transportation, and other project allies teamed up to secure federal funding for the project's public benefits at Tower 55. Funding from all contributors will be used to install additional trackage, improve track alignment, enhance signals, build new structurally improved bridges, and improve pedestrian safety and viability. Overall, these changes will improve the air quality and overall mobility in the North Texas region.

Since 2008, BNSF has worked with freight customers that have built 63 new or expanded facilities in Texas, creating more than 880 jobs and investing $620 million.

Improving Texans' Way of Life

BNSF is committed to consistently supporting and enhancing the quality of life in communities where its employees work and live. Many BNSF employee teams in Fort Worth regularly hold service days, which provide a chance for them to get involved in their community and provide assistance to local nonprofit agencies. Such activities and contributions from the BNSF Railway Foundation have benefited scores of local organizations.

BNSF is also proud of its track record in hiring military veterans. Since 2005, BNSF has hired more than 4,000 U.S. military veterans. Locally, BNSF supports veterans as a sponsor of the annual Armed Forces Bowl held at Texas Christian University. This annual bowl game, played at TCU's Amon G. Carter Football Stadium, benefits the Wounded Warrior program, an organization whose mission is to support wounded service members and help them adjust to civilian life.

BNSF and the more than 4,500 employees who live and work here are proud to call Fort Worth home and be part of this vibrant and growing community— today and into the future.

Learn more at www.BNSF.com.

Dallas/Fort Worth International Airport

Dallas/Fort Worth (DFW) International Airport has emerged as one of the world's most highly regarded airports, connecting the nation's fastest-growing metropolitan area with nonstop air service to five continents.

Nestled on 17,000 acres of land between the cities of Dallas and Fort Worth, Texas, DFW International Airport now ranks as the fourth-busiest airport based on flight operations, and eighth-busiest in terms of passengers, serving travelers with top-notch facilities that provide an optimal travel experience.

In less than four decades of existence, Dallas/Fort Worth International Airport has grown into a "global super hub" for airline activity, with a goal of delivering an unparalleled airport environment for its passengers. The world has noticed. For five consecutive years, DFW has achieved a top five ranking among large airports worldwide for excellence in customer service, a distinction that has placed it among the finest airports in the world, according to Airports Council International surveys of international passengers. DFW achieves this level of excellence by paying close attention to the needs of all of its customers, from passengers to airlines and business partners.

The true mark of success for DFW Airport can be measured in the breadth of air service it provides to its community. DFW boasts nonstop flights to more than 190 destinations worldwide, including about 50 international destinations. With 160,000 passengers visiting DFW every day, the airport strives to meet and exceed the high expectations of the traveling public without the complications and hubbub of overcrowded airports.

As a leading transportation hub, DFW serves a powerful economic driver for both Dallas and Fort Worth. The bustling DFW aerotropolis pumps over $16 billion into the Dallas/Fort Worth region annually and supports up to 300,000 jobs either directly or indirectly.

Cargo continues to be a key contributor to DFW's success by providing Dallas/Fort Worth with additional connections to the emerging global economies in Asia as well as the capacity to ship goods around the globe. As evidenced by the successful International Cargo Centre complex, DFW's cargo business is highly tuned to the demand for time-sensitive freight deliveries. In addition to its outstanding facilities and available capacity to expand, DFW has immediate connectivity to five major highways for convenient access to many domestic markets, and its central location in the United States means shippers can fly goods into DFW and then rapidly on to a wide range of destinations.

(Re)defining Your Airport

As part of its goal to enhance every aspect of the airport experience for its passengers, DFW has embarked on a seven-year program to upgrade and renew its original four terminal buildings. The Terminal Renewal and Improvement Program, or TRIP, a $2.3 billion project, will (re)define DFW Airport for the next 40 years. Additionally, the program engages the community in a diverse and meaningful way, creating more than 2,000 jobs in design, construction, and contracting.

In the coming years, passengers will notice welcome enhancements starting on arrival at the airport's enhanced entry plazas and garages. Inside the terminals, DFW is modernizing everything from ticketing to security checkpoints, shopping and dining options and passenger flow. Perhaps more important, the renovations mean faster flow through security, check-in, and baggage claim, thanks to a combination of user-friendly technology and DFW's own brand of personalized Texas hospitality.

A Leader in Sustainability

With more than a decade of adopting environmentally sensitive business practices, DFW has developed a robust and comprehensive Sustainability Program focused on environmental stewardship, along with responsible management of energy, waste, water, and other resources. By embracing a business culture focused on social responsibility in addition to the bottom line, DFW shows its leadership for sustainability, not only in the airport industry but among public entities worldwide.

DFW's vehicle fleet has been almost completely converted to clean burning compressed natural gas over the past 15 years, saving DFW millions in fuel costs and cutting the airport's carbon emissions by more than 95 percent. New plumbing fixtures in bathrooms across all five airport terminals have cut DFW's customer water usage by 50 percent, saving about 5.5 million gallons of water each month. Currently about 30 percent of DFW's annual electric usage is wind generated, and that number is growing as DFW seeks more renewable sources of energy.

DFW's holistic approach on environmental stewardship has consistently resulted in significant cost savings, ultimately leading to facilities that are green, efficient, cost-effective, and traveler-friendly. At DFW, delivering one of the best travel experiences in the world now goes hand-in-hand with reducing the Airport's environmental footprint. For additional information, visit www.dfwairport.com.

This page, from left: DFW International Airport's Terminal D is home to flights connecting 49 international destinations to Dallas/Fort Worth. Terminal D opened in 2005 to worldwide acclaim and features much of DFW's Art Program. DFW International Airport is regarded as one of the world's top airports for overall customer service. For five consecutive years, DFW has ranked among the world's top five airports for customer service among large airports worldwide in passenger surveys conducted by Airports Council International.

The T (Fort Worth Transportation Authority)

Whether the mode is bus, train, trolley, or future commuter rails, and whether the destination is downtown or the other side of the globe by way of the Dallas/Fort Worth International Airport, The T is in the business of bringing people together.

The hub of one of the fastest-growing large U.S. counties, Fort Worth will see more changes in public transportation over the next 10 years than since The T's creation in 1983, when residents approved a half-cent sales tax for public transit.

Today The T is a regional transportation authority of the state of Texas, governed by a nine-member board of directors appointed by the Fort Worth City Council and Tarrant County. It annually provides transportation to nearly nine million passengers on buses; vans for the mobility impaired; vanpools; and the Trinity Railway Express (TRE), the existing commuter railroad between Fort Worth and Dallas. With buses that operate on compressed natural gas, The T has been a national leader in the use of clean transportation. The T is also very committed to the Fort Worth community, taking leadership roles in development, partnering with organizations and businesses, and tailoring services around special events.

The T's headquarters are at the Hershel R. Payne Transportation Complex at 1600 East Lancaster Avenue. It also hosts public activities at the community room of its downtown Intermodal Transportation Center (ITC) at 9th and Jones Streets, where it brings together major modes of passenger ground transportation in one centralized, convenient downtown location. In addition to The T's local bus and TRE service, the ITC serves Amtrak, Greyhound regional bus lines, rental cars, taxis, customer amenities, and concessions.

This page, above: As a supporter of air quality, The T's bus fleet operates on compressed natural gas and encourages bicycles on bus racks and trains. This page, bottom right: The Trinity Railway Express carries 8,500 riders a day between Fort Worth and Dallas.

Catch TEX Rail, a new commuter rail starting in southwest Fort Worth that will travel through downtown, across Tarrant County to Grapevine, and into Dallas/ Fort Worth International Airport. Or hop an even newer train to events at Texas Motor Speedway or a job at Alliance Texas, with future connections into Denton. Watch service on the "Spur" East Lancaster enhanced bus corridor morph into a Southeast Fort Worth rail line that someday could travel as far as Arlington. These concepts for expanded passenger travel options are part of the 25-year strategic vision of the Fort Worth Transportation Authority (The T) to make public transportation more rapid, more regional, and with more rail.

TEXRail

With the western side of the Dallas–Fort Worth Metroplex projected to soon have the highest levels of traffic congestion in north-central Texas, The T stands ready to help. The T is committed to partnering with the City of Fort Worth, Tarrant County, and the region to help alleviate increased congestion through strategic expansion and enhancement of public transportation options.

For more information, visit The T's Web site at www.the-t.com.

PROFILES OF COMPANIES AND ORGANIZATIONS
Tourism and Hospitality

Worthington Renaissance Fort Worth Hotel

For over three decades, the Worthington has lived up to its reputation as Fort Worth's original AAA Four-Diamond luxury hotel. Located in the heart of downtown, overlooking historic Sundance Square, this distinctive Marriott Renaissance® property is considered to be "The Star of Texas" by countless travelers.

Above, from left: Located in the heart of Fort Worth, the hotel is known for its impeccable Texas-style service and gracious hospitality. BarWired, the hotel's Internet Cafe, provides a comfortable lounge overlooking downtown. The Terrace Suite has a spectacular skyline view.

From the very beginning, the magnificent Worthington Renaissance Fort Worth Hotel was conceived with luxury in mind. Originally called the Americana, it was built over three city blocks in 1981 as part of the major Downtown Fort Worth revitalization, and immediately garnered the Automobile Association of America's (AAA) coveted Four-Diamond rating—the city's first to achieve that distinction.

Its unique, pyramid-stepped silhouette makes a dramatic impact on the skyline and provides stunning views of dynamic Sundance Square—a 35-block commercial, residential, entertainment, and retail district in the heart of Downtown Fort Worth. Designed by 3D International in Houston, Texas, the opulent hotel was lavishly renovated in 2007 by architect David M. Schwarz.

A top destination in Fort Worth for business and leisure travel, the Worthington Renaissance is convenient to many of the attractions that make Fort Worth such an exciting metropolis to visit, live, and do business. It is located just minutes from the famed Fort Worth Stockyards, Dallas/Fort Worth International Airport, the Convention Center, Cowboys Stadium, Bass Hall (home to the Fort Worth Symphony Orchestra, Texas Ballet Theater, and Fort Worth Opera), the Museum District, Texas Motor Speedway, Amon Carter Museum, Texas Christian University (TCU), and hundreds of popular dining, entertainment, and cultural establishments.

Artfully balanced and thoughtfully designed, the Worthington Renaissance has the right amenities to make guests feel at home. Twelve floors feature 504 sumptuous

guest rooms, including 30 Terrace or Balcony suites and a Concierge Level for the ultimate luxury experience. Classic Western-style elegance is reflected in each room's tasteful décor, while the furnishings provide exceptional comfort and modern functionality, with high-speed Internet access, Marriott Plug-In technology panels, spacious desks, ample lighting, and in-room coffee and tea. Like many Marriott properties, the hotel has a comprehensive smoke-free policy to protect the health of its guests.

When it comes to meetings, conferences, weddings, and other business or social events, the Worthington provides outstanding service. Twenty-one wired meeting rooms and a 10,530-square-foot Grand Ballroom add up to 57,000 square feet, accommodating a range of groups in a variety of configurations. There is also an 11,000-square-foot terrace for outdoor receptions. Event menus with elegant catering are available for everything from casual receptions to black-tie extravaganzas.

Business travelers are supported with a full-service business center offering copy, fax, and messenger services, network/Internet printing, and overnight delivery/pickup, and wireless high-speed Internet in guest rooms and public areas, in addition to the Wired-for-Business in-room option.

With three restaurants on-site and dozens more nearby, Worthington Renaissance guests have many dining alternatives. Vidalias, which offers a fresh, unique perspective on authentic Southwestern cooking, is one of downtown's most popular fine dining spots for breakfast, lunch, or dinner.

The Lobby Bar, featuring classic American food, is the perfect place to unwind with friends or colleagues, watch a sports event, or enjoy a Yellow Rose Martini, a house specialty. BarWired is a chic Internet cafe, bar, and lounge serving Starbucks coffee and a wide selection of other beverages for its online and offline customers. All three hotel restaurants have a casual dress code.

It's easy for travelers to stay in shape at the Worthington Fitness Center, complete with free weights, cardiovascular equipment, tennis courts, and a Sport Court® for multiple recreational activities. Swimmers will appreciate the indoor pool, whirlpool, and sauna. Massage services are also available by appointment.

For more information about the Worthington Renaissance Fort Worth Hotel, visit www.marriott.com or call (817) 870-1000.

This page, from left: Named for the famous American pianist who achieved worldwide recognition in 1958 when he won the International Tchaikovsky Piano Competition, the Van Cliburn suite offers the best view of downtown and Sundance Square. The hotel's spacious residential-like guest rooms are designed for all travelers and feature flat-screen TVs, comfortable bedding and easy high-speed Internet access. The Renaissance hotel offers myriad dining options for every taste.

The Fort Worth Club

From cozy guestroom accommodations and world-class cuisine to an Athletic Center and unique events, The Fort Worth Club is a premier social, business, and athletic venue that strives to meet and exceed the ever-changing expectations and needs of its membership.

The 11th Floor—"the members' floor"—provides a relaxing escape for busy members, with multiple dining choices in a luxurious setting. The Library serves as a full-service, upscale bar and restaurant with dining and comfortable lounge seating with a view of downtown Fort Worth.

Other dining options at The Fort Worth Club include The Grille, a popular family, breakfast, and business lunch spot for casual dining in an inviting atmosphere. The Heritage Room offers a quiet, intimate setting, whether for an important business meeting or romantic dinner for two. Sports-themed amenities, including flat-screen TVs, card tables, a pool table, and billiards memorabilia, are found at the Davey O'Brien Sports Lounge. Cuisine at The Fort Worth Club is overseen by Tim Prefontaine, who beat out 61 other regional teams at the 2008 American Culinary Federation Regional Team USA to win the gold medal.

The club's Athletic Center offers cardio and strength training equipment; fitness classes; an indoor heated lap pool; squash, racquetball, and basketball courts; and much more. A staff of certified fitness professionals provides personalized instruction.

This page, above: The Library serves as a full-service, upscale bar and restaurant, offering a beautiful view of downtown Fort Worth. This page, right: The Fort Worth Club Athletic Center offers world-class cardio and strength training equipment and fitness classes, including indoor cycling.

In 1885 the Commercial Club was founded as a prestigious gathering place for business and community leaders to socialize and work for the continued growth of Fort Worth.

Renamed The Fort Worth Club in 1906, this illustrious organization erected a 12-story building featuring apartment suites for prominent members in 1926. Club President Amon G. Carter hosted many distinguished guests in his personal quarters, including President Franklin D. Roosevelt, Bob Hope, and Gene Autry.

Those suites were transformed into the Inn at the Club, 21 boutique guest rooms catering to members, club tenants, corporate groups, wedding parties, or those looking for a "home away from home" in beautiful downtown Fort Worth.

The Fort Worth Club serves as a lavish venue for all types of events, from business luncheons to elegant wedding receptions. The club's catering department and creative culinary team can help to plan and execute an event that will exceed all expectations.

For additional information, visit www.fortworthclub.com.

The Fort Worth Convention & Visitors Bureau

In Fort Worth, "cowboys and culture" isn't just a tagline—it's a way of life. Nowhere else can you find a destination that is so quintessentially Texas, beautifully preserved through the Stockyards National Historic District and Sundance Square and enriched by the Cultural District, in addition to unique major-league entertainment and sports. With a population of more than 750,000, Fort Worth was recently voted one of "America's Most Livable Communities."

Fort Worth is the rare city that celebrates both cowboys and culture in big Texas style. Once a rough-and-tumble frontier town, Fort Worth began as a dusty and lawless home to the brave soldier, the frontiersman, and the outlaw. Today the Fort Worth Convention & Visitors Bureau has the pleasure of promoting Fort Worth as one of the largest cities in Texas, the 16th-largest city in the United States, and one that revels in its uniqueness as an internationally acclaimed tourism destination.

Fort Worth celebrates its Western heritage every day as a way of life, including attractions such as the Fort Worth Herd, the annual Fort Worth Stock Show and Rodeo, Billy Bob's Honky-Tonk, and year-round rodeo at Stockyards Championship Rodeo.

Early Fort Worth proponents also had the vision to establish the city as the top cultural destination in the Southwest. The Cultural District is home to five world-class museums—the Kimbell Art Museum; the Amon Carter Museum of American Art; the Modern Art Museum of Fort Worth; the Fort Worth Museum of Science and History; and the National Cowgirl Museum and Hall of Fame.

With a reputation for being safe and friendly, Fort Worth makes a perfect getaway for families as well. The Fort Worth Zoo is ranked as a top-five zoo in the nation, and close proximity to major-league attractions such as Texas Motor Speedway, Rangers Ballpark, Cowboys Stadium, and Six Flags makes Fort Worth the ideal vacation destination.

As you can imagine, tourism is bustling, with more than 5.5 million visitors per year and an economic impact exceeding $1.345 billion. Tourism employs more than 17,000 industry workers, and the city is widely known for its warm hospitality. The Fort Worth Convention & Visitors Bureau works on behalf of the city to drive leisure tourism as well as meetings and conventions, which provide a positive and immediate impact on the health of the city.

The Fort Worth Convention Center and Will Rogers Memorial Center are superior convention facilities, both known for their breathtaking architecture, convenience, and location. The state-of-the-art convention center is located in the heart of downtown and adjacent to the renowned Philip Johnson Water Gardens, offering an amazing integrated city experience for guests.

For more information on meeting venues, unique spaces, and accommodations, go to MeetInFortWorth.com. Visitors planning a trip to Fort Worth can go to FortWorth.com to book a hotel and find discounts and events to plan their trip.

Above: The Trinity River reflects the lights of the Fort Worth skyline.

Omni Fort Worth Hotel

The newest star in the Lone Star State, the Omni Fort Worth Hotel features a casual yet sophisticated style that is as gracious and dynamic as Fort Worth itself.

Guestrooms and Suites

The Omni Fort Worth Hotel's 614 luxurious guestrooms and suites feature natural linens, plush bedding with saddle blanket throws, three different types of pillows, and white noise machines to ensure that guests have a restful night's sleep. High-speed Internet-ready workstations have wireless Internet. The handsomely appointed Deluxe Rooms, located on the hotel's top floors, afford superior views of the city.

Stately Suites offer 690 square feet, with a gorgeous living area and king bed, an upgraded bathroom, and a parlor area with a half bath, bar counter, pullout sofa bed, and small table. Hospitality Suites feature an attractive open layout of 894 square feet with wet bar and balcony. Luxury Suites, at 1,276 square feet, feature a striking living area with a pullout sofa bed and comfortable rocking chair, king bedroom with luxury bathroom, dining room, half bath, and large work area. Two sliding doors open from the dining room onto a spacious outdoor balcony.

Even more luxury is found on the top floors of the hotel, where the 1,636-square-foot Presidential Suites feature multiple sitting areas, a sectional sofa, a lavish wet bar, and a dining area that can accommodate up to six. A large work area boasts an executive desk and gorgeous wood panel shelves. Along with a highly upgraded bathroom, there is a second full bath with a walk-in shower. Sliding glass doors lead to a spacious 402-square-foot balcony.

The sumptuous, 1,825-square-foot Omni Suite encompasses two entrances offering access to either the living area or entertainment room. The expansive living area houses a large TV armoire, sectional sofa, writing desk, and several plush chairs. The entertainment room has a TV, marble-top wet bar, poker setup for four players, and foosball table. The formal dining room seats eight comfortably. The master suite contains a highly upgraded bathroom and walk-in closet. A full-size guest bathroom with roll-in shower is located by the suite's second entrance.

Above, from left:
The Omni Fort Worth Hotel is located in the city of "Cowboys and Culture," conveniently located within walking distance to Sundance Square, restaurants, and nightlife. Bob's Steak and Chop House is a nationally renowned steak house specializing in corn-fed, Midwestern prime beef.

Conveniently located in the heart of downtown Fort Worth, adjacent to the Fort Worth Convention Center, the Omni Fort Worth Hotel is sculpted from native stone and rich hardwoods and wrapped in glass. With its open, inviting spaces and modern amenities, the hotel was voted the "Best New Hotel" by both staff and readers and "Best View of the City" by readers in *Texas Magazine*'s 2009 "Best of Fort Worth." In addition, Omni Fort Worth Hotel was named a top 100 meeting hotel by Cvent in 2012. Omni Hotels and Resorts was named highest in hotel guest satisfaction and was highest among nine upper-upscale hotel brands according to J.D. Power and Associates 2012 North American Hotel Guest Satisfaction Index Survey. In addition to providing a stellar overall lodging experience, the Omni Fort Worth Hotel offers a choice location, and is a regular stop for Molly the Trolley, which provides convenient service to most downtown attractions.

Accessible rooms are available for guests who need ADA features such as enlarged door openings, and a roll-in shower and toilet with grab bars.

Dining and Spa

The Omni Fort Worth offers a wide range of dining options, Bob's Steak & Chop House, a nationally renowned steak house, specializes in the finest corn-fed, Midwestern prime beef. The Cast Iron, the hotel's casual restaurant, was named the Best Hotel Restaurant in the *Fort Worth, Texas: The City's Magazine*'s 2009 through 2011 Culinary Awards. Whiskey & Rye, a relaxed neighborhood sports bar, was named the Best Bar Food by *The City Magazine* and one of the Top 5 Places for a Drink in Fort Worth by *The Cowtown Chronicles*. Wine Thief features a wide selection of wines paired with the finest cheeses. The Water Horse Pool Bar offers a full-service bar with a poolside menu, HDTVs, and satellite music.

The Mokara Spa in Fort Worth offers a full range of spa treatments from massages, facials, and body wrap treatments to manicures and pedicures. For the ultimate pampering, guests can sample one-of-a-kind spa treatments with a Western twist.

Choose from a sweet tea body gloss or the wildly popular Texas Pecan Manicure or Pedicure. The hotel also features a fully equipped fitness center and an outdoor pool.

Meetings and More

With 29 meeting rooms and 68,000 square feet of meeting space, the Omni Fort Worth is ideal for conventions, meetings, and other events. The Texas Ballroom, with 18,878 square feet, puts South Fork to shame. The 9,576-square-foot Fort Worth Ballroom is well-suited for a wedding or other special occasion. Built-in pre-function areas, 6,500 square feet of usable outdoor space, state-of-the-art audiovisual services, and catering services are also available.

Located atop the Omni Fort Worth, the Omni Residences provide the ultimate in luxury and service. Offering full access to the hotel, the residences feature top-of-the-line amenities and exquisite designer touches in traditional, transitional, or contemporary style. All residences have a spacious private balcony offering spectacular views of downtown Fort Worth. For more information or reservations, visit www.omnihotels.com.

Clockwise from above left: Sculpted from native stone and rich hardwoods and wrapped in glass, the Omni Fort Worth Hotel is an exciting venue; at every turn, you'll experience the true nature of Fort Worth, from rustic to refined. The Mokara Spa pampers guests with a world-class spa experience. The Wine Thief is a secluded yet inviting wine bar where guests gather to enjoy wine selections paired with only the finest cheeses.

PHOTO CREDITS

Unless otherwise indicated, all images are listed left to right.

Page ii: © Denis Tangney, Jr.
Page v: © Ken Slade
Page vi: © L Clarke/age fotostock
Page x: © David Liu
Page 2, left: © John Elk III/Alamy
Pages 2-3: © Sylvain Grandadam/age fotostock
Page 3, right: © LS Photos/Alamy
Page 4, left: © Cliff Baise
Pages 4-5: © Cliff Baise
Page 5, right: © Jeff Stvan
Page 6, left: © SuperStock
Pages 6-7: © Thomas Hawk
Page 7, right: © Q-Images/Alamy
Page 8, left: © ZUMA Press, Inc./Alamy
Pages 8-9: © Ray Carlin/Icon SMI/Corbis
Page 9, right: © Aflo Co. Ltd./Alamy
Page 10, left: © Q-Images/Alamy
Pages 10-11: © Larry Sallee
Page 11, right: © Jill Stephenson/Alamy
Page 12, left: © Shubroto Chattopadhyay/Corbis
Page 12, right: © North Wind/North Wind Picture Archives
Page 13: © Arthur Rothstein/Corbis
Page 14, left: Courtesy, Library of Congress
Page 14, right: Public domain
Page 15: © Carolyn Brown
Page 16: © John J. Buckley
Page 18: © Cliff Baise
Page 19: © SuperStock
Page 20, left: © AP Photo/Matt Slocum
Page 20, right: © AP Photo/LM Otero
Page 21: © Steven Martin
Page 22: © Tim Pannell/Corbis
Page 23: © Lynne Jacobs

Page 24: © Gyro Photography/aman
Page 25: © Jim Peipert
Page 26, left: © LS Photos/Alamy
Page 26, right: © Wildroze Photography
Page 27: © Jeremy Woodhouse/age fotostock
Page 28: © Ralph Lauer/ZUMAPRESS.com
Page 29: © Tom Vrotsos
Page 30: © Wade Griffith
Page 31, left: © Glenn Killman
Page 31, right: © Justin Terveen
Page 32: © David Woo/Corbis
Page 33: © Glenn Killman
Page 34, left: © Brad Nicol/Alamy
Page 34, right: © Sergio Piumatti
Page 35: © FOTOSEARCH RM
Page 36: © William Harding
Page 37: © Brad Nicol/Alamy
Page 38, left: Courtesy, Lone Star Nightclub. Photo provided by Lone Star Attitude Band.
Page 38, right: © Gabe Grote
Page 39: © LS Photos/Alamy
Page 40: © Danita Delimont/Alamy
Page 41: © SuperStock
Page 42, left: © Ray Carlin/Icon SMI/Corbis
Page 42, right: © ZUMA Press, Inc./Alamy
Page 43: © Michael Prengler/Cal Sport Media via AP Images
Page 44: © Ralph Lauer/ZUMAPRESS. com
Page 45, left: © Glenn Killman
Page 45, right: © Ralph Lauer/ZUMAPRESS.com
Page 46: © Q-Images/Alamy
Page 47, left: © John Syphrit
Page 47, right: © Ralph Lauer/ZUMAPRESS.com
Page 48: Courtesy, Rosales + Partners

cherbo publishing group, inc.

TYPOGRAPHY

Principal faces used: Univers, designed by Adrian Frutiger in 1957;
Helvetica, designed by Matthew Carter, Edouard Hoffmann,
and Max Miedinger in 1959

HARDWARE

Macintosh 8-core Intel desktops, digital color laser printing with
Xerox Phaser 7400, DocuColor Proofer

SOFTWARE

QuarkXPress, CS6 (In Design, Adobe Illustrator, Adobe Photoshop, Adobe Acrobat),
Microsoft Word, Eye-One Match by X-Rite, FlightCheck by Markzware

PAPER

Text Paper: #80 Luna Matte

Bound in Rainbow® recycled content papers from
Ecological Fibers, Inc.

Dust Jacket: #100 Sterling-Litho Gloss